Handbook for the Newbery Medal and Honor Books

1990–1999

Gale W. Sherman & Bette D. Ammon

Alleyside Press

Fort Atkinson, Wisconsin

Published by Alleyside Press,
an imprint of Highsmith Press LLC
Highsmith Press
W5527 Highway 106
P.O. Box 800
Fort Atkinson, Wisconsin 53538-0800
1-800-558-2110

Copyright © by Gale W. Sherman and Bette D. Ammon, 2000
Cover design: Debra Neu Sletten

The paper used in this publication meets the minimum requirements of the
American National Standard for Information Science - Permanence of Paper
for Printed Library Material. ANSI/NISO Z39.48-1992.

Library of Congress Cataloging-in-Publication Data
Sherman, Gale W.
  Handbook for the Newbery Medal and Honor books, 1990-1999 / Gale W.Sherman,
Bette D. Ammon.
      p. cm.
Ammon's name appears first on the earlier edition.
Includes bibliographical references and index.
  ISBN 1-57950-046-3 (alk. paper)
1. Children's literature, American--Study and teaching (Elementary)--Handbooks,
manuals, etc. 2. Reading--United States--Aids and devices--Handbooks, manuals, etc.
3. Teaching--Aids and devices--Handbooks, manuals, etc. 4. Newbery Medal--
Bibliography. 5. Caldecott Medal--Bibliography. I. Ammon, Bette DeBruyne. II. Title.
  LB1575.5.U5 A46 2000
    810.9'9282--dc21   00-008324

Contents

Introduction

Since 1922, when the Newbery Award was first established, the winners and honor designees have helped define excellence in fine children's literature. Just as books published during Newbery's time reflected his society's view of children and what they should know and learn, the 36 Newbery Medal and Honor Books of the 1990s reveal a good deal about current standards for children's books and contemporary lives for children.

Although there are numerous awards for superior and popular children's books distributed regularly in the United States, there is no greater honor (or guarantee of success) than the Newbery and Caldecott Medals. Indeed, in an era where children's book titles occupy space on bestseller lists, the writing, publishing, and reading of quality books for children has achieved even more prestige and importance. In addition, the sheer numbers of books published each year make the evaluation, selection, and use of books a challenging endeavor.

The Handbook for the Newbery Medal and Honor Books, 1990–1999 is intended specifically for librarians, teachers, and other readers who are involved in children's literature and interested in promoting lifelong reading habits. Here is a chance to put to use those Newbery Medal and Honor Books sitting on the shelves of nearly every library. In addition, parents who are committed to raising readers will find useful information to enhance their children's reading experiences.

Biographical information about John Newbery, the history the Newbery Award and Medal, and an explanation of the nominating and voting process is included. In addition the authors provide definitions and explanations of the *Handbook*'s format designed for use by librarians, teachers and parents who have a limited amount of time to collect in-depth information for the nominated titles.

Bibliographic data is included for each book, including publications in other formats. Additionally, genre(s), theme(s), readability and interest data, review sources, author information, plot summaries, tips for classroom use, a booktalk (Book Clip), curriculum connection and extension ideas, and a list of six titles of similar interest are listed for each book. The appendices provide resources for further information about the Newbery Award and the process of nomination and voting. A complete listing of all Newbery Medal and Honor winners is also included.

Newberys in the Classroom

Using literature and "real books" in classrooms make the Newbery Medal and Honor books a natural pre-selected list for classroom use. If librarians and classroom teachers present and utilize these titles in a lively and interesting manner, their students will experience and enjoy some of the finest literature available. Even though some may disagree with the selected titles, none can argue with the diversity and fine quality of these 36 titles that represent children's literature of the 90s. John Newbery would undoubtedly be astounded by the numbers and varieties of books honored in his name, not only in the 90s, but also throughout the past 78 years.

Today's young readers can find enchantment, enlightenment, and entertainment by reading these Newbery Medal and Honor books. If we are indeed interested in creating lifelong proficient readers, it is imperative that we provide students with numerous occasions to read and experience diverse, quality literature. Utilizing these Newbery winners within a classroom reading curricula can easily become one of these opportunities.

Newbery and the Award

John Newbery, the Man

A self-educated farmer's son, John Newbery (1713–December 22, 1767) is credited with being the originator of published juvenile literature. He was born in

Waltham St. Lawrence, Berkshire, England, and except for a brief stint at the local village school, Newbery received no formal education. However, he loved reading and this fortunately made up for his lack of schooling.

At the age of seventeen, Newbery became an assistant to William Carnan who was the owner and editor of a local newspaper, *The Reading Mercury.* When Carnan died several years later, he bequeathed the newspaper to his brother and Newbery. Eventually Newbery married Carnan's widow and made the decision to expand his business. In 1744, he opened a warehouse in London and one year later, in St. Paul's Churchyard, launched his bookshop called The Bible and the Sun. Here he became well known as a writer, publisher, bookseller, and vendor of patent medicines. Apparently, much of Newbery's income came from the sale of these medicines and he often advertised them in some of his most famous children's stories. The father in Newbery's *Goody Two Shoes* dies a terrible death, "seized with a fever in a place where Dr. James' powder was not to be had."

During the next fifteen years, Newbery began several newspapers and magazines. His journals published Dr. Johnson's *Idler* essays and Oliver Goldsmith's *Citizen of the World.* Authors knew Newbery as a good friend who was always available for a small advance. In Goldsmith's *Vicar of Wakefield,* he describes a bustling bookseller based on Newbery as a "red-faced, good-natured little man who was always in a hurry."

Newbery's chief accomplishment, however, was that of becoming the first publisher who made children's books an important part of a publishing enterprise. Before his time, literature for children was scanty. Newbery's belief in pleasing children as well as instructing them opened a new field of literature. A disciple of John Locke, he believed in educating children but thought the "pill should be sugared."

The publication of Newbery's Juvenile Library allowed children's books a more lasting form than the popular chapbooks of that period. The Library consisted of a series of tiny books bound attractively in gilt and flowered paper. Newbery spared no expense—the paper, printing and binding were of the finest quality available. The books were designed to appeal to the young reader and included titles such as *The History of Little Goody Two Shoes, Tommy Trip and His Dog Jowler*, and *The Renowned History of Giles Gingerbread.* Exactly who wrote some of these books is a mystery since they were all published anonymously. However, Newbery himself undoubtedly wrote and planned many of them, and probably enlisted the help of Goldsmith, Giles Jones, and Dr.

Johnson. He commissioned numerous books to meet the demands of the growing middle class population. These parents desired books that would please, instruct, and amuse their offspring.

Highly energized writing, the use of Dutch paper covers, and the touting of his other products characterized the style of Newbery's publications. Newbery was one of the most blatant and ingenious advertisers of his time. In *Blossoms of Morality*, one chapter opens "My dear papa," said young Theophilis to his father. "I cannot help pitying those poor little boys whose parents are not in a condition to purchase them such a nice gilded library as that with which you have supplied me from my good friends at the corner of Saint Paul's Churchyard."

Newbery's books were original in style, written with good intent, and published for the education and amusement of children. Called "a friend of children" and "perhaps the first bookman to appreciate the reading interests of children," John Newbery does indeed appear to be the appropriate individual to have his name attached to "the most distinguished" publications for young people.

History of the Newbery Award

In 1921, during a speech made to the Children's Librarians' Section of the American Library Association (ALA), Frederic Melcher (co-editor of *Publishers Weekly* and president of R.R. Bowker), spontaneously proposed a book award to be sponsored by this group. He wondered whether those librarians as a group would "take on one more job, by helping to assure a greater literature for children as well as a wider reading of the available literature.... They could help build a greater literature by giving authoritative recognition to those who wrote well." Melcher later said he thought of the plan on the spot and presented it along with the suggestion "that good old John Newbery's name be attached to the medal."

The reason Melcher requested the award be named after John Newbery was because of Newbery's dedication to promoting reading for children. Melcher said "this lovable book-seller and publisher of eighteenth-century London, was perhaps the first bookman to appreciate that the reading interests of children were worthy of especial and individual attention."

Melcher's concept was enthusiastically accepted and approved. The first Newbery Medal was presented to Hendrik Willem van Loon for *The Story of Mankind* (Liveright, 1921) in 1922. The following year, Melcher composed a four-point statement detailing the origin, method, and purpose of the award to be adopted by ALA.

1. The author must be a citizen or resident of the United States.
2. Reprints and compilations were not to be considered.
3. The work must be original.
4. The work need not be written solely for children.

In 1932, the rule concerning originality was defined further to encompass books traditional in origin that were "the result of individual research, the retelling and reinterpretation being the writer's own." In addition, it was resolved that a previous recipient of the Newbery Medal could receive another Newbery award only when receiving the unanimous vote of the Newbery Committee. The rationale behind this resolution was to encourage innovative work by new writers. However, this was rescinded in 1958 because the necessity to foster new authors and illustrators no longer existed. At that time committee members were reminded that the award was for the book and not the author.

The Medal

Melcher financed the medal and engaged the services of the young, but already noted sculptor, René Chambellan. Melcher recommended the medal reflect the intent of the award showing "genius giving of its best to the child." The face of the medal portrays three figures: the central image is that of a man holding a book, representing the writer. On either side are pictured a boy and a girl with hands held out to the author "as if to receive his creative talents." The opposite side of the Medal depicts an open book with the words "For the most distinguished contribution to American literature for children." Around the edges are the words "John Newbery Medal" and "Awarded annually by the Children's Librarians' Section of the American Library Association." Melcher donated the medal for the winner and since his death in 1963, his son Daniel Melcher has continued to provide the award.

The medal itself is struck in bronze, and in 1956 it was agreed that gold facsimile seals of the medal would be placed on the winning books. Since 1971 silver facsimile seals, with the designation "Newbery Honor Book" have been made available for the Honor Books. These seals can be purchased from the Association for Library Service to Children (ALSC). All profits from these sales go to the Frederick G. Melcher Scholarship fund.

The Process

Initially when the Newbery Medal was awarded, title selec-

tions were made by a popular vote of the Children's Librarians' Section (CLS) of ALA. After three years, in 1924, the Book Evaluation Committee of this Section decided a popular vote was not dependable enough to choose the most distinguished contribution of the year. They established the Newbery Committee, and by 1929, decided the members would total fifteen. Members of CLS were invited to submit recommendations for the most estimable books to the committee, with final selection resting in the hands of the Newbery Committee.

From 1937 to 1978 the Newbery - Caldecott Committee had twenty-three members. In 1978 the Children's Services Division of ALA was renamed the Association for Library Service to Children (ALSC). At that time, the bylaws were changed, creating two separate committees with fifteen members each. From a slate of no fewer than fourteen, the general membership elects seven members each year. A chairperson is elected annually from a slate of two and the vice-president (president-elect) appoints the other seven committee members.

Until 1933, the number of votes each title received on the last ballot was made public, but since then the individual book discussions, ballots and tallies have been kept confidential. Prior to 1958, the voting for the Newbery award was done by mail but from 1958 to date, voting has taken place at the ALA Midwinter Conference. Since 1933 the number of ballots, tallies, and discussions have been made confidential.

For the whole year preceding the balloting, the committee members read, reread, and evaluate the books published that year and nominated by fellow committee members and the membership of ALSC. Before they take a vote in committee, each nominated book (one by one) is discussed. Generally a consensus reveals the time has come for the initial ballot. Each committee member votes for three books. The first choice receives four points, second choice—three points, and third choice—two points. Since the committee numbers fifteen members, a book must have a minimum of eight first place rankings to win. Additionally, this title needs an eight-point lead over the book receiving the next highest number of points.

If there is not a winner when the results of the first ballot are announced, the committee starts again with their discussion. Any titles that received no votes on the first ballot are eliminated. This procedure continues until there is a winner according to the numerical ratings noted above.

Honor Books

When the Newbery Award was first established, the committee released the names of the "runners-up" books. These were titles that remained the longest in the voting procedure. The term "runners-up" was changed to Honor Books in 1971.

Before 1977, Honor Books were listed based on the number of votes they received on the final ballot. In 1977 the ALSC Board gave the Newbery Committee more direction for determining Honor Books. "Following the selection of the Caldecott or Newbery Medal winner, the Committee, if it chooses to name Honor Books, may ballot once again among the books that appeared on the final Medal-winning ballot. The Committee may elect to name one or more of the books that are highest in this balloting as Honor Books." For this, the Committee may choose between balloting again and selecting the next-highest books on the winning ballot as Honor Books. If that is the case, they have to decide the number of titles to name as Honor Books.

The Committee may choose to ballot again and in this instance, the only books which may appear on the new ballot are the titles that received points on the award-winning ballot. After this voting, the Committee agrees upon the number of titles to be included as Honor Books. There is no set number of Honor books and the Committee is instructed to keep in mind that the "books should be truly distinguished, not merely general contenders." The Honor Books have been announced in alphabetical order by author since 1964.

The Announcement

Initially the Newbery Medal was presented at the summer ALA conference and the voting results were confidential until that time. In 1949, the announcements began to be made after the voting was completed (at ALA's mid-winter meeting) with the formal presentations of the awards done at ALA's summer conference. Postings of the winners appear almost immediately following the announcement on ALSC's website: www.ala.org/alsc/newbery.html. The winner of the Newbery Medal is honored at a banquet and presented with the Medal. His/her speech is delivered at that time (along with that of the Caldecott Medal winner) and recordings of these speeches are presented to the banquet attendees.

The prestige and influence of the Newbery Award cannot be overstated. Since the institution of the award in 1921, children's book publication has been tremendously stimulated. Parents, teachers, and librarians (as well as children) pay attention to these books. Most importantly,

standards and guidelines in evaluating literature for children have been established as a result. One of Mr. Melcher's goals, that of helping to "build a greater literature by giving authoritative recognition to outstanding authors," has been achieved by the Newbery Award program.

How to Use This Handbook

The *Handbook* is organized to give users access to a variety of information about each title.

Bibliographic Data

When a title is available in another format such as paperback and audiotape, that information is included here.

Genre(s)

This Newbery list includes many literature genres. For a book to fit into a specific genre, it must have certain characteristics. However, often books can be categorized in two or more genres. It is important to place each title in as many genres as is appropriate. This permits the viewing of the book with a wider perspective and provides additional opportunities for use of the book. The following definitions will help explain genre divisions.

Adventure: Action-packed books in authentic settings with daring characters facing unbelievable odds, larger-than-life situations, and/or cunning villains.

Animal Stories: Books in which the central characters are animals. The human characters are often secondary.

Biography: A biography is a factual accounting of a person's life. For children, biographies make real the lives of people who have been significant contributors to the world.

Contemporary Realistic Fiction: Literature dealing with authentic incidents which could happen to real people living in our present society.

Fantasy: Literature taking place in a time and setting in which the impossible becomes convincingly possible. Usually an element of magic and/or the supernatural exists and sometimes maps are included.

Historical Fiction: Fictionalized accounts with generally accurate descriptions of how people lived at certain times in certain places. The stories may be based on real events or people, but details of action and conversation are fictitious. An "autobiographical novel" may be included within this genre.

Humor: Funny or hilarious incidents designed to appeal to an intended audience.

Informational Books: These nonfiction works present accurate facts and information about the past, present, and future of the world in which children live. While useful for reports, this genre can also provide a pleasurable reading experience.

Mystery: Suspense-filled stories with enough clues given to hold the reader's interest and provoke discovery of "who did it?"

Multicultural: Literature about minority ethnic groups with diverse values and characteristics.

Poetry: A rhythmic combination of words that can inspire imagination.

Science Fiction: Often referred to as "speculative fiction," science fiction includes advanced, unknown technology.

Short Stories: A collection of individual writings each featuring a limited number of characters focusing on a single incident or event. Some stories may be longer than others, and some collections may have a unifying theme.

Sports: Stories dealing with topics of sportsmanship, technical details of individual sports, and/or relating the playing of sports to some aspect of life.

Traditional Literature: Literature based on oral traditions such a fables, myths, legends, folktales, and epics.

Theme(s)

The inclusion of multiple themes is provided to enhance the book's potential classroom use and to help match books with readers.

Readability

Two independent readability evaluations were performed for each title using the Fry Readability Scale. This scale reflects reading levels for instructional materials, and recreational reading usually lags a year behind the instructional level. Keep this in mind when matching a book with a struggling reader. Look for books with a lower readability in order to create a successful reading experience.

There are a variety of readability scales, which combined with subjective use, may offer slightly different results.

Therefore, in some instances, reading level information presented by individual book publishers, reviewers, and *Children's Books in Print* does not necessarily coincide with this Handbook's readability information. All data on readability is offered solely as a guide and individual judgement is recommended.

Interest Level

Interest and readability levels often do not match. The subject matter of individual books often determines the audience and interest level may transcend the reading level. In order to expose children to a wider variety of literature, adults should use the interest level determinations to help them select appropriate books to read aloud.

Reviews

Review citations are listed for each title. These provide users with diverse opinions and sometimes additional information about specific books. These critical reviews can help teachers and librarians develops rationales and plans for the classroom use of these books.

Plot

The plot details have been kept to a minimum. Additional information can be determined from the following sections: theme(s), book clips, and Curriculum Connections.

Tips

This section offers additional insight into introducing the book to readers. Frequently reading aloud a portion of the book is recommended; sometimes particular information about the book's format is provided.

Some titles are perfect for reading aloud in their entirety, other books are less appropriate to read aloud and may be more suitable for individual reading experiences.

Related Tips provide additional sources on the Internet, in other teaching resources, or in periodicals.

The Author

Children often are intrigued by details about authors' lives, so brief author information is included. If available, specific information about the author and the writing of this Newbery Award book is included in a second paragraph.

The citation for the complete text of the winning author's acceptance speech will be listed here as well as Related Author Resources such as author biographies, videos, and appropriate websites.

Book Clip

Booktalks are an excellent way to introduce books and hook potential readers. They aren't book reviews or reports—simply a preview of the pleasures to come. Choosing an appropriate read-aloud passage from the book using the author's own unique language may be the best inducement a booktalker can employ.

Curriculum Connections

Specific ideas for integrating these books in classroom curricula are included in this section. Most of these suggestions are suitable for independent literature extensions and can replace traditional boring book reports. These implementation suggestions can be modified according to the developmental/grade level of the reader or listener.

Some students might choose to read one of the Newbery winners based on the curriculum connection that interests them the most.

Related Internet sites are listed following each curriculum connection. The sites provided were all up and running when accessed in May 2000.

Keep on Reading

For students who wish to read similar books, this section lists six books of comparable appeal. These may include picture books, novels, biographies and nonfiction books, and the readability levels may vary widely among the recommended titles. The index cross-references all titles mentioned in this *Handbook*, making it simple for adults who are trying to match readers with other books they will love. Pairing kids with books is a natural way to encourage enjoyable reading and give students an opportunity to develop those reading muscles.

1990

MEDAL

Number the Stars

Lois Lowry

Plot Summary

Ten-year-old Annemarie Johansen and her best friend
Ellen Rosen are terrified by the German soldiers who
patrol the streets in German occupied Denmark during
World War II. When the news comes out that Jews are
being rounded up by the Nazis, Ellen's parents flee and
Annemarie's family pretends Ellen is another daughter
while they arrange for her escape from a fishing village
where Jews are being smuggled to freedom in Sweden.
A scared but resolute heroine, Annemarie bravely
delivers a handkerchief (coated with blood and cocaine to
deaden the search dogs' sense of smell) to her uncle just
before the Nazi soldiers search his boat.

Tips

Number the Stars is an excellent choice for reading
aloud. The seventeen short chapters include headings
that give clues to what is about to occur. Because
Number the Stars is set around the Jewish New Year
(Rosh Hashanah through Yom Kippur), it could easily be
read aloud during this period in September through
October. Prior to reading this book, provide students with
geographical information about Europe—specifically,
Denmark's size and location in relation to Germany and
Sweden.

Related Tips

Number the Stars by Lois Lowry (Scholastic, 1997)

Number the Stars by Kathy Jordan (Teacher Created,
1993)

"Getting a Grip on World War II" by Dorothy Dobson
Instructor 104(6):40 Mar 1995

www.smplanet.com/bookclub/interactive/archive/stars
3.98/starsintro.html

www.carolhurst.com/titles/numberthestars.html

http://online.coled.mankato.msus.edu/dept/ci/matz/
rdgwld/Books/Numberthestars.html

www.ed.uiuc.edu/YLP/96-97/96 97_curriculum_units/
Holocaust_KO'Malley/lit_series.html

www.mcdougallittell.com/lit/litcon/number/guide.htm

Author Information

Born in Hawaii and now living in Boston, Lowry has
been a freelance writer since 1972. She writes from

Just the Facts

LC 88-37134. 160p. 1989. $16 (ISBN 0-395-51060-0).
Houghton Mifflin.

Paperback. 144p. 1998. $4.50 (ISBN 0-440-22753-4).
Bantam.

Audio book. Unabridged, 3 hrs., 30 min. 1993. $23 (ISBN
1-55690 856-3). Recorded Books.

Video. 15 min. 1994. PBS Video.

Genres: historical fiction, multicultural

Themes: Jews, Denmark, World War II, Holocaust,
German occupation, Danish Resistance Movement, terror,
courage, friendship, secrets, smuggling, loyalty, death,
family relationships, Sweden

Readability: Fifth grade

Interest Level: Fourth through sixth grade

Review Citations:

Booklist 85(13):1194 Mar 1, 1989

Bulletin of the Center for Children's Books 42(7):176
Mar 1989

Horn Book 65(3):371 May/June 1989

Publishers Weekly 235(8):234 Feb 24, 1989

School Library Journal 35(7):177 Mar 1989

Wilson Library Bulletin 64(3):95 Nov 1989

childhood memories and her own experiences as a parent. Her success at writing realistically about many different topics, humorous and intense, is due to her desire to help readers deal with important issues.

Number the Stars is based on the childhood of Lowry's friend Annelise, who grew up in Copenhagen. In 1988, Lowry took a vacation with Annelise. It was the first uninterrupted visit they had ever had and they "talked and talked and talked." Lowry says that for the first time she began to understand "that historic events and day-to-day life are not separate things." *Number the Stars* includes information about Denmark told to Lowry by Annelise, as well as other details gleaned from Lowry's own visit to that country. She saw a pair of shoes made from fish skins and thought: "Oh, they're so ugly and [she] put the ugly shoes, and the child's reaction, into the book." Annelise's memory of the German soldiers was simple: "I remember the high shiny boots."

Related Author Resources

Looking Back: A Book of Memories by Lois Lowry (Walter Lorraine, 1998).

Lois Lowry by Lois Markham (Learning Works, 1995) www.scils.rutgers.edu/special/kay/lowry.html www.mtnbrook.k12.al.us/wf98/llowry.htm www.randomhouse.com/teachers/guides/lowr.html www.ipl.org/youth/AskAuthor/Lowry.html

Newbery Acceptance Speech: *Horn Book Magazine* 66(4):412-424 July/Aug 90

Book Clip

In Lois Lowry's *Number the Stars* Annemarie has been entrusted with a critically important mission. The package she is carrying must be delivered to her uncle's fishing boat before he leaves with his secret cargo of Danish Jews on their flight to freedom.

> Annemarie stopped, suddenly, and stood still on the path. There was a turn immediately ahead. Beyond it, she knew, as soon as she rounded the turn, she would see the landscape open to the sea. The woods would be behind her there, and ahead of her would be the harbor, the docks, and the countless fishing boats. Very soon it would be noisy there, with engines starting, fishermen calling to one another, and gulls crying. But she had heard something else. She heard bushes rustling ahead. She heard footsteps. And—she was certain it was not her imagination—she heard a low growl. Cautiously, she took a step forward.

> And another. She approached the turn in the path, and the noises continued. Then they were there, in front of her. Four armed soldiers. With them, straining at taut leashes, were two large dogs, their eyes glittering, their lips curled. (page 112, hardback edition)

Nazi soldiers with guns, snarling dogs, secret packages— and Annemarie is only ten years old.

Curriculum Connections

History (Codes, Cryptography, Communication, Resistance, Military)

Codes were used as part of the Resistance movement and by the military as an intelligence tool. Students can learn codes, make up their own, or simply read more about them. Provide books like: *The Ultimate Spy Book* by H. Keith Melton (Dorling Kindersley, 1996); *Codes Ciphers and Other Cryptic and Clandestine Communications: 400 Ways to Send Secret Messages from Hieroglyphs to the Internet* by Fred B. Wrixon (Black Dog, 1998); *How to Keep a Secret: Writing and Talking in Code* by Elizabeth James, Carol Barkin and Joel Schick (Lothrop, Lee & Shepard, 1998); *How to Write and Decode Secret Messages* by Marvin Miller (Scholastic, 1998); *The Cat's Elbow and Other Secret Languages* by Alvin Schwartz (Farrar, Straus & Giroux, 1988); *The Code Talkers: American Indians in World War II* by Robert Daily (Franklin Watts, 1997); *Unsung Heroes of World War II: The Story of the Navajo Code Talkers* by Deanne Durrett (Facts on File, 1998).

Related Websites

Navajo Code Talkers: World War II Fact Sheet
http://history.navy.mil/faqs/faq61-2.htm

Cryptology Lessons
www.achiever.com/freehmpg/cryptology/lessons.html

History (Holocaust, World War II, Research, Internet)

The Internet can provide students with informative visual and written information about the Holocaust to complement print resources. The following websites are especially helpful in relation to *Number the Stars:*

Related Websites

Cybrary of the Holocaust
http://remember.org/

United States Holocaust Memorial Museum
www.ushmm.org

Children of the Holocaust
   www.wiesenthal.com/children/prvchild.htm
Holocaust Curriculum Resources for K-12
   http://falcon.jmu.edu/~ramseyil/holo.htm
Danish rescuer of Jews tells story of simple humanity
   http://jewishsf.com/bk951020/sfadane.htm

Social Studies (Newspapers, Resistance Fighters)

Using the Danish Resistance movement as a starting point, expand the study of similar movements to include underground newspapers, Radio Free Europe, and other specific national resistance groups. Consider using *Anne Frank Remembered: The Story of the Woman Who Helped to Hide the Frank Family* by Miep Gies (Simon & Schuster, 1988); *Darkness over Denmark: The Danish Resistance and the Rescue of the Jews* by Ellen Levine (Holiday House, 1999); *A Time to Fight Back: True Stories of Wartime Resistance* by Jayne Pettit (Houghton Mifflin, 1996); and *'Vive La France': The French Resistance During World War II* by Robert Green (Franklin Watts, 1997).

Related Websites

Resisters, Rescuers, and Bystanders: A Guide for Teachers
   http://remember.org/guide/wit.root.wit.res.html
October 1943 – The Rescue of the Danish Jews from Annihilation 'Endlosung' in Europe
   www.denmark.org/denmark/rescue.html
Women of Valor: Partisans and Resistance Fighters
   www.interlog.com/~mighty/valor/bios.htm

Keep on Reading

In My Hands: Memories of a Holocaust Rescuer by Jennifer Armstrong (Knopf, 1999). A young nursing student schemes to protect and hide the local Jews during the Holocaust.

Sky: A True Story of Resistance During World War II by Hanneke Ippisch (Simon & Schuster, 1996). As a young teenager, Hanneke Ippisch becomes a member of the Dutch resistance movement and helps transport Jews to safe hiding places.

Shadow of the Wall by Christa Laird (Beech Tree Books, 1997). While living in the Warsaw Ghetto, Misha joins a resistance organization.

Greater Than Angels by Carol Matas (Simon & Schuster, 1998). Brave citizens in Vichy, France, risk their lives to save Jewish refugees during World War II.

The Final Journey by Gudrun Pausewang (Puffin, 1998). After hiding for two years in a basement, Alice Dubsky finds herself on a train bound for Auschwitz.

Hide and Seek by Ida Vos (Houghton Mifflin, 1991). This novel tells the story of a Jewish family and their experiences during the Nazi occupation of Holland.

1990

HONOR

Afternoon of the Elves
Janet Lisle

Plot Summary

Hillary is a proper nine-year-old—she and her two best friends wear matching outfits, and she has loving parents and an immaculate backyard. But when Sara-Kate (her strange misfit neighbor with the disheveled clothes, spooky dark house, and unkempt yard) invites her over to see an elf village, Hillary cannot resist. Prickly Sara-Kate seems to know everything about elves. In fact, Hillary begins to suspect that Sara-Kate herself is a member of that tiny population. But what Sara-Kate is unwilling to share is information about her secluded and ill mother. Hillary learns about magic and friendship as she's drawn into the elf world by Sara-Kate.

Tips

There are two times during the calendar year when this book would be especially appropriate to read aloud—in September when the book's action begins, or around St. Patrick's Day with respect to elves and other little people. The fifteen chapters are broken into smaller segments, which make it easy to tailor read-aloud sessions to imme-diate needs. Sharing this book may foster discussion concerning compassion and acceptance of differences among people.

Author Information

Janet Taylor Lisle grew up an avid reader in rural Connecticut. A writer of stories since she was a child, Lisle vividly remembers feeling like an outsider when she went to a private school in sixth grade. Following her graduation from Smith College and a stint as a VISTA volunteer, Lisle attended journalism school and spent the next ten years writing news and feature stories. However, after the birth of her child, Lisle began writing for children.

Writing *Afternoon of the Elves* proved to be an intense experience for Lisle. Enchanted with the idea of secret worlds and shy communities, she believes that individuals are always looking beyond the ordinary and rarely satis-fied with "logical answers."

Just the Facts

LC 88-35099. 128p. 1989. $15.95 (ISBN 0-531-05837-9). Orchard Books/Watts.

Paperback. 1991. $3.99 (ISBN 0-590-439944-8). Scholastic.

Audio book. Unabridged, 3.5 hours. 1995. $26 (ISBN 0-788-70396-2). Recorded Books.

Genre: contemporary realistic fiction

Themes: miniatures, elves, mental illness, loneliness, compassion, love, imagination, friendship, peer relationships, school life, secrets, fear, trust, independence, curiosity, survival

Readability: Sixth grade

Interest Level: Fifth through seventh grade

Review Citations:

Booklist 85(22):1979 Aug 1989

Bulletin of the Center for Children's Books 43(2):37 Oct 1989

Horn Book Magazine 65(5):622 Sept/Oct 1989

Publishers Weekly 236(2)78 July 14, 1989

School Library Journal 35(13):254 Sept 1989

Wilson Library Bulletin 64(7)53 Mar 1990

Book Clip

Nine-year-old Hillary has been intrigued by Sara-Kate's supposed elf village in her backyard. But Sara-Kate can be so difficult sometimes—it's hard to be friends with her.

> Two days later, Hillary had put the elf village almost completely out of her mind when Sara-Kate appeared at her elbow in the hall at school. She appeared so suddenly, and at such an odd time—all the other fifth graders were at sports—that Hillary jumped. Sara-Kate leaned toward her and spoke in a high, breathless voice. "Where have you been? I thought you were coming again. The elves have built a playground. They have a swimming pool and a Ferris wheel now." She flung a string of hair over her shoulder and smiled nervously. "You should come see," she told Hillary. "A Ferris wheel!" In spite of herself, Hillary felt a jab of excitement. "How did they build that?" "With Popsicle sticks and two bicycle wheels. It really goes around. The elves come out at night and play on it. Really and truly," said Sara-Kate, looking into Hillary's eyes. "I can tell it's been used in the morning." (pages 13–14, hardback edition)

Hilary can't resist another peek at this wonderful elf village. Would you like to see it? Then you need to spend an *Afternoon* with *the Elves*.

Curriculum Connections

Art (History of Art, Miniatures, Museum Collections, Artists)

Many museums periodically feature displays of miniature scenes or buildings. If possible, arrange a field trip to view such a display or point students to the websites below for virtual tours. Students can look at other miniatures by looking at catalogs that can be borrowed from craft stores.

Related Websites

Museum of Science and Industry: Colleen Moore's Fairy Castle
    http://msichicago.org/exhibit/fairy_castle/fchome.html

Toy and Miniature Museum of Kansas City
    www.umkc.edu/tmm/

Delaware Toy and Miniature Museum
    www.thomes.net/toys/

Art (Crafts, Creativity, Miniatures)

Using a variety of materials, students may wish to construct a small elf village of their own. Lisle's depiction of the elves' Ferris wheel (page 18, hardback edition), along with the cover illustration, provides enough information so students should be able to build it easily. Invite a miniaturist to discuss this popular craft and display items. Many communities have organized groups who meet regularly to work together and students can take a look at the website below to find out if there is a group in your area.

Related Websites

National Association of Miniature Enthusiasts
    www.miniatures.org/

Writing (Language Arts, Creative Writing)

Give students the choice of writing about either of the following quotations from *Afternoon of the Elves:* "Have you ever wondered what it would feel like to be an elf?" (page 19, hardback edition). Or students can look more analytically at the world around them, the way Sara-Kate advises Hillary: "You can't just stomp around the place expecting to be shown things. Go slowly and quietly, and look deep." (page 44, hardback edition).

Keep on Reading

Behind the Attic Wall by Sylvia Cassedy (Crowell, 1987). Neglected Maggie discovers a tiny family who lives behind the wall in the attic.

The Village by the Sea by Paula Fox (Orchard Books, 1988). Emma and her new friend build a small village on the beach.

Margo's House by Peni R. Griffin (Margaret McElderry, 1996). While Margo's father recovers from a heart attack, she discovers that the doll house and dolls he made for her have come alive.

Tom's Midnight Garden by A. Philippa Pearce (HarperCollins, 1992). An English boy is transported to a magical and wonderful garden where he finds a new friend.

Elfsong by Ann Warren Turner (Harcourt Brace, 1995). Maddy discovers a magical forest where elves have lived for centuries.

The Mennyms by Sylvia Waugh (Greenwillow, 1994). A family of life-size rag dolls lives carefully in an English neighborhood.

1990

HONOR

The Winter Room
Gary Paulsen

Plot Summary

Eldon and Wayne are two brothers growing up on a remote northern Minnesota farm in the 1930s. Their day-to-day lives are filled with hard work and hard earned joys. Long winter evenings are spent listening intently to stories that reveal the family's history and amazing details concerning their elderly uncle.

Tips

In the first three pages entitled "Turning," Paulsen focuses on how a writer's words create definite moods for readers. This section also specifically sets the stage for *The Winter Room*. However, this chapter will have more appeal to adults than to young readers. Though not hilarious like Paulsen's *Harris and Me* (Harcourt, 1993), this slim novel is reminiscent of farm scenes and adventurous boys. Either read the book aloud in its entirety (skipping "Tuning"), or read through the "Spring" section to introduce the story.

www.westga.edu/~kidreach/Brian'sWinter.html

Author Information

Gary Paulsen has tried almost every career in existence but always comes back to writing, and at this point he has over 130 titles to his credit. As a child of a career military father, he moved around constantly, never living for more than five months in one spot. His childhood was not happy; he had no friends, didn't do well in sports, and wasn't very successful in school. While in high school, he discovered the public library and began to read voraciously. After four years of service in the army, Paulsen worked in the aerospace industry and discovered he had writing talent. Now living in New Mexico, Paulsen continues to research his writing by experiencing everything firsthand. He is the 1997 winner of the Margaret A. Edwards Award honoring his lifetime contribution to young adult readers.

Related Author Resources

Gary Paulsen by Stephanie True Peters (Learning Works, 1999)

Eastern Sun Winter Moon: An Autobiographical Odyssey by Gary Paulsen (Harcourt Brace, 1993)

Just the Facts

LC-89-42541. 1989. 103p $15.95 (ISBN 0-531-1-05839-5). Orchard Books.

Paperback. $4.50 (ISBN 0-440-40454-1). Bantam Doubleday Dell.

Audio book. Unabridged, 2 hours. 1994. $19 (ISBN 0-788-70011-1). Recorded Books.

Genre: historical fiction

Themes: farm life, families, brothers, seasons, life cycles, death, woodcarving, logging, storytelling, Norwegian Americans, immigrants

Readability: Fifth grade

Interest Level: Fourth through seventh grade

Review Citations:

English Journal 81(1):85 Jan 1992

Bulletin of the Center for Childrens Books 43(5):118 Jan 1990

Horn Book Magazine 66(2):209 March 1990

Publishers Weekly 236(13):69 Sep 29, 1989

School Library Journal 35(14):136 Oct 1989

Wilson Library Bulletin 64(3):94 Nov 1989

Video: *Trumpet Video Visits Gary Paulsen.* Color, 24 min. The Trumpet Club, 1993.
www.randomhouse.com/features/garypaulsen/
www.ipl.org/youth/AskAuthor/paulsen.html
http://falcon.jmu.edu/~ramseyil/paulsen.htm
www.scils.rutgers.edu/special/kay/paulsen.html
http://borg.lib.vt.edu/ejournals/ALAN/fall94/Schmitz.html

Book Clip

Eldon and Wayne loved the long winter evenings when Uncle David told meandering stories about his days long ago as a logger.

> The stories were just there, not something to be questioned and opened up. Uncle David just told them and they came from him and went into us and became part of us so that his memory became our memory. But nothing about them was ever questioned. Until he told the story that broke things. (page 84, paperback edition)

It was Uncle David's story "The Woodcutter" that was beyond belief for the boys. How can the telling of it break things?

Curriculum Connections

Social Studies (Logging--History, Contemporary Issues)

Uncle David tells the boys about the old days when the forests were thick with giant Norway pines before the logging camps cut them all down. He said

> "It was sad and most of us wished we hadn't done it ...." (page 89, paperback edition)

The decimation of old growth forests has been a continuing concern to preservationists. Students can learn more about this and other logging issues by reading further. Applicable books include the picture book *Giants in the Land* by Diana Applebaum (Houghton Mifflin, 1993); *Bull Whackers to Whistle Punks: Logging in the Old West* by Sharlene Nelson and Ted W. Nelson (Franklin Watts, 1996); and *Rough and Ready Loggers* by A.S. Gintzler (John Muir Publications, 1996).

Related Websites

Old-Growth Forests in the United States Pacific Northwest
www.wri.org/biodiv/b011-btl.html

John Muir Exhibit
www.sierraclub.org/john_muir_exhibit/index_noframes.html

VanNatta Logging History Museum of Northwest Oregon
www.aone.com/~robert/histlog.html

Early Logging Practices
http://wwwgen.bham.wednet.edu/muselogg.htm

Arts and Crafts (Quilts and Quilting)

Quilts, like the ones Uncle David and Nels use, often become cherished family heirlooms. To help students appreciate the value of old family quilts, share *The Keeping Quilt* by Patricia Polacco (Simon & Schuster, 1994), which celebrates the history of a quilt made by her great-great grandmother who emigrated from Russia. If possible, display a historic quilt and invite the owner to tell its story.

Other picture books to share include *Tar Beach* by Faith Ringgold (Crown, 1991); *Sweet Clara and the Freedom Quilt* by Deborah Hopkinson (Knopf, 1993); and *Stitching Stars: The Story Quilts of Harriet Powers* by Mary E. Lyons (Scribner, 1993).

Invite local quilters to share their creations. Some students might be interested in creating a small sample pattern or class quilt. Books of interest include *Kids Making Quilts for Kids: Young Person's Guide for Having Fun while Helping Others* (NTC, 1995); *Quilting Activities across the Curriculum* by Wendy Buchberg (Scholastic, 1997); *Kids Can Quilt* by Barbara J. Eikmeier (Martingale, 1997); Ann Whitford Paul's *Eight Hands Round: A Patchwork Alphabet* (HarperCollins, 1991) which contains the origins of 26 early American quilting patterns; and *The Quilt-Block History of Pioneer Days: With Projects Kids Can Make* by Mary Cobb (Millbrook, 1995).

Related Websites

American Quilts
www.pbs.org/americaquilts/

Quilt History Links
www.womenfolk.com/grandmothers/qhlinks.htm

Quilt Resources with Sweet Clara
http://people.whitman.edu/~hopkinda/QUILT%7E1.HTM

Design a Quilt
www.ti.com/calc/docs/act/unquilt.htm

Literature (Storytelling)

Every winter evening, the family gathers to listen to Uncle David, who is a riveting storyteller. Students may be interested in learning and practicing this artform, and then performing their stories for others. Invite a storyteller from your community to teach the basics. Other resources include *The Storyteller's Cornucopia* by Cathie Hilterbran Cooper (Alleyside, 1998); *Every Child a Storyteller* by Harriet R. Kinghorn and Mary Helen Pelton (Libraries Unlimited, 1991); Caroline Feller Bauer's *Read for the Fun of It: Active Programming with Books for Children* (Wilson, 1992); *Storytelling for Young Adults: Techniques and Treasury* by Gail de Vos (Libraries Unlimited, 1991); *Storytelling: Process and Practice* by Norma J. Livo and Sandra A. Rietz (Libraries Unlimited, 1986); and *Twice upon a Time* by Judy Sierra and Robert Kaminski (Wilson, 1989). Some students may wish to learn tales and stage a storytelling festival for elementary schools or public libraries.

Related Websites

National Storytelling Network
   www.storynet.org/

Aaron Shepard's Storytelling Page
   www.aaronshep.com/storytelling/

Storytelling Lesson Plans and Activities
   www.storyarts.org/lessonplans/

Handbook for Storytellers
   http://falcon.jmu.edu/~ramseyil/storyhandbook.htm

Keep on Reading

Liar by Winifred Morris (Walker, 1996). A troubled four-teen-year-old is sent to live with his gruff grandfather and loving grandmother on their farm.

Shiloh by Phyllis Reynolds Naylor (Macmillan, 1991). Marty rescues a mistreated dog and keeps him a secret on the family farm.

Harris and Me: A Summer Remembered by Gary Paulsen (Harcourt Brace, 1993). An eleven-year-old boy experiences farm life during the summer he spends with Harris and his family.

A Day No Pigs Would Die by Robert Newton Peck (Knopf, 1972). A young adult novel featuring coming of age on a Vermont farm.

Soup series by Robert Newton Peck (Knopf). Stories of the author's misadventures in rural Vermont during the 1920s.

The Sin Eater by Gary S. Schmidt (Lodestar/Dutton, 1996). Moving to his grandparents' farm after his mother's death, Cole finds a new life.

1990

HONOR

Shabanu, Daughter of the Wind
Suzanne Fisher Staples

Plot Summary

The life and customs of nomadic camel herders in the Cholistan desert in modern-day Pakistan are richly portrayed in this book. Independent and free-spirited, eleven-year-old Shabanu is close to her nomadic family but resistant to the idea of an arranged marriage, especially to settle a feud. Ultimately she has to decide whether she is willing to sacrifice her personal liberty in order to preserve her family's safety and status.

Tips

Girls, especially, will be interested in this gripping story of a young woman's life in a very different culture. Best suited for independent reading, *Shabanu, Daughter of the Wind* will appeal to confident readers who will utilize the glossary, list of characters, and map. *Haveli* (Knopf, 1993) continues Shabanu's story.

Related Tips

www.harperchildrens.com/schoolhouse/TeachersGuides/SFSindex.htm

www.etc.sccoe.org/i98/tier2/Tier2info/jordan/web page3/index.html

www.foxsden.org/psf/projects/shabanu/shabanu.htm

www.scils.rutgers.edu/childlit/feb97/0028.html

Author Information

Suzanne Fisher Staples was raised in Pennsylvania and grew up loving books. Her grandmother bribed her with stories in exchange for rock garden work. That was when Staples decided to become a writer. Working as a journalist for the Agency for International Development, Staples was in Pakistan in 1985. She was studying the cycle of poverty, with a particular focus on women. While in the Cholistan desert, Staples developed a friendship with an eleven-year-old girl who became her inspiration for the character Shabanu in this first novel.

Related Author Resources

www.ridgenet.org/event/staples.htm

Different Is Just Different by Suzanne Fisher Staples
http://scholar.lib.vt.edu/ejournals/ALAN/winter95/Staples.html

Just the Facts

LC-89-02714. 1989. 240p. $18.99 (ISBN 0-394-84815-7). Random House.

Paperback. $4.99 (ISBN 0-679-81030-7). Random House Sprinters.

Audio book. Unabridged, 7 hours. 1995. $42 (ISBN 0-7887-0189-4). Recorded Books.

Genres: contemporary realistic fiction, multicultural

Themes: Pakistan, obedience, nomads, coming-of-age, repression, marriage--arranged, desert life, gender roles, Muslims, birth and birthing, revenge, camels, physical development, families, duty, honor, independence, death, grief, dowries

Readability: Sixth grade
Interest Level: Seventh through twelfth grade
Review Citations:
English Journal 79(8):78 Dec 1990
Horn Book Magazine 66(1):72 Jan/Feb 1990
New Yorker 65(41):144 Nov 27, 1989
Publishers Weekly 236(14):55 Oct 13, 1989
School Library Journal 35(15):128 Nov 1989
Wilson Library Bulletin 64(9):8 May 1990

What Johnny Can't Read: Censorship in American Libraries by Suzanne Fisher Staples
   http://scholar.lib.vt.edu/ejournals/ALAN/winter96/pubCONN.html

Book Clip

Eleven-year-old Shabanu is her father's helper and goes with him every year to the fairground where camels are sold. Riding their prize camel, Guluband, Shabanu travels...

> ... down the main avenue of the fairground, past rows and rows of animals and men sitting on empty oxcarts talking prices. They all look up to see such a fine animal, and I lift my chin and look straight ahead. I think this, even more than the carnival, is what I look forward to from year to year. How I'll miss it next year. I try to imagine myself a veiled woman with a family of my own. A shiver steals across my shoulders. (page 50, paperback edition)

Within one short year Shabanu will be married to a man her father chooses and her independent life will be over. How will she bear it?

Curriculum Connections

History (Nomads, Tribal Life, Desert Life)

Various cultures and countries throughout time have supported nomadic tribal life with families, like Shabanu's, traveling from place to place with the seasons. Provide students with opportunities to learn more. Books of interest include: *Deserts* by Martin Jenkins et al. (Lerner, 1996); *Nomads* by Donna Bailey (Steck-Vaughn, 1990); *Desert Places* by Robyn Davidson (Viking, 1996); *Greener Pastures: Politics, Markets, and Community among a Migrant Pastoral People* by Arun Agrawal (Duke University, 1999); and *Living Spaces in the Desert* by Gail Stewart (Rourke, 1989).

Related Websites

CIA. The World Factbook (explore by countries)
   www.odci.gov/cia/publications/factbook/

Images of Afghanistan in 1976–78
   http://geogweb.berkeley.edu/GeoImages/Powell/PowellAfghan.html

The Negev Bedouin: A Photographic Exhibit
   http://medic.bgu.ac.il/bedouin/bedouin.html

Odyssey Online: Near East-People
   www.emory.edu/CARLOS/ODYSSEY/NEAREAST/people.html

Art and Life in Africa Online: Fulani Information
   www.uiowa.edu/~africart/toc/people/Fulani.html

Literature (Classroom Library, Coming of Age, Girls/Women, Multicultural)

Assemble a collection of books featuring girls who come of age in other times and/or other lands. Include *Catherine, Called Birdy* by Karen Cushman (Clarion, 1994); *A Girl Named Disaster* by Nancy Farmer (Orchard, 1996); *Habibi* by Naomi Shihab Nye (Simon & Schuster, 1997); *Bat Mitzvah: A Jewish Girl's Coming of Age* by Barbara Diamond Goldin (Viking, 1995); *One More River* by Lynne Reid Banks (William Morrow, 1992); Suzanne Fisher Staples' *Shabanu: Daughter of the Wind* (Knopf, 1989) and *Haveli* (Knopf, 1993). See Keep on Reading below for more suggestions.

Sociology (Customs, Islam, Muslims, Women's Issues, Women's Rights, Current Events)

Women's rights within Shabanu's culture are very different from those of most American women. Some students will want to learn more about current and past customs in other Arab cultures. Specific issues to research include clothing requirements and restrictions (veils, head covers, etc.), nomadic life, jobs and educational opportunities for women, arranged marriages, honor killings for sexual impropriety, and women in politics—including Pakistan's former prime minister Benazir Bhutto.

Related Websites

Women in Islam
   www.answering-islam.org/Women/inislam.html

The Middle East Institute: The social system and morality of Islam
   www.mideasti.org/library/islam/social.htm

UNICEF's Voices of Youth New Girls' Rights
   www.unicef.org/voy/

Compton's Encyclopedia Online: BHUTTO, Benazir
   www.optonline.com/comptons/ceo/00533_A.html

Women, Islam & Equality
   www.iran-e-azad.org/english/book_on_women.html

Keep on Reading

The Bedouin's Gazelle by Frances Temple (Orchard, 1996). Set in the fourteenth century, this tale is about

Bedouin cousins who are betrothed at birth.

I Rode a Horse of Milk White Jade by Diane Lee Wilson (Orchard, 1998). A strong-willed Chinese girl has adventures in the time of Kublai Khan.

Wise Child by Monica Furlong (Random House, 1989). Apprenticed to a healer, Wise Child grows to maturity and wisdom through a diverse education and unusual experiences.

Shadow Spinner by Susan Fletcher (Atheneum, 1998). A brave young girl risks nearly everything in her effort to find a story's ending for the famous storyteller, Scheherazade.

The Storyteller's Beads by Jane Kurtz (Gulliver Books, 1998). While on a dangerous journey, two young Ethiopian girls overcome their cultural differences.

So Far from the Bamboo Grove by Yoko Kawashima Watkins (Beech Tree, 1994). At the end of World War II, eleven-year-old Yoko escapes from Korea and returns to her Japanese homeland.

1991
MEDAL
Maniac Magee
Jerry Spinelli

Plot Summary

Maniac Magee is a legend. He can run faster, kick farther, and untie knots better than anyone. But Maniac has no home. Adopted for a while by the kindly Beale family, Maniac leaves when his white presence in their all black neighborhood brings trouble to his adopted family. His next "home" is the bandshell near the zoo. Maniac lives with Grayson, an old minor league baseball player who never learned to read. Maniac teaches him and, though their time together is short, it is full of discovery and love. On the move again, Maniac continues to touch the lives of all who know him—black and white, young and old.

Tips

The 46 chapters vary in length from two to five pages and can be easily combined to suit read-aloud schedules. The cover will be enticing after the story is known. Many readers will want to read it on their own after hearing it read aloud. Jim Trelease recommends this book as a great read-aloud.

Related Tips

A Guide for Using Maniac Magee in the Classroom by Michael Levin (Teacher Created Materials, 1995)
Maniac Magee by Jerry Spinelli (Scholastic, 1997).
www.mcdougallittell.com/lit/litcon/maniac/guide.htm
www.d64.k12.il.us/Dist64/Dist/maniacmagee.htm
www.eduplace.com/tview/tviews/tijero1.html
www.carolhurst.com/titles/maniacmagee.html

Author Information

Jerry Spinelli was born in Norristown, Pennsylvania. He and his wife, Eileen (also a writer) have six children. One of his first writing experiences was writing a poem after his high school football team won a big game. It was published in the local newspaper and Spinelli has been writing ever since. His first book, *Space Station Seventh Grade,* was not intended as a young adult novel, but Jason's story of his thirteenth year accidentally pushed Spinelli into the YA field. He is interested in writing for children of various ages.

Jeffrey, the maniac in *Maniac Magee,* is a composite of many elements from Spinelli's life. He has a friend who

Just the Facts

LC 89-27144. 192p. 1990. $15.95 (ISBN 0-316-80722-2). Little, Brown.
Paperback. 1991. $5.95 (ISBN 0-06-440424-2). HarperTrophy.
Audio book. Abridged, 2.5 hours. 1993. (ISBN 1-882-209s10-9). Pharaoh Audiobooks.
Video. 30 min. AIMS Media, 1992.
Genres: contemporary realistic fiction, multicultural, humor
Themes: homelessness, racism, prejudice, sports, friendship, illiteracy, families, home, independence, hope, love, orphans, heroes, baseball, legends, storytelling
Readability: Fifth grade
Interest Level: Fifth through ninth grade
Review Citations:
Booklist 86(19):1902 June 1, 1990
Horn Book Magazine 66(3):340 May/June 1990
Publishers Weekly 237(1):260 May 11, 1990
School Library Journal 36(6):138 June 1990

grew up in an orphanage and at age eight discovered his black skin did make a difference. That old friend began running and "he ran everywhere he went." Spinelli recalls a baseball coach who would throw his special pitch once to each player—the stop ball. Spinelli met "Amanda Beale" several years ago on a school visit. A teacher there introduced him to a girl "who carried her entire home library to school in a suitcase, because she could not bear to abandon her books to the crayons and sharp teeth of her siblings and pets at home."

Related Author Resources

Knots in My Yo-Yo String: The Autobiography of a Kid by Jerry Spinelli (Knopf, 1998).

Jerry Spinelli by Kimberley Clark (Learning Works, 1999).

Video: *Good Conversation! A Talk with Jerry Spinelli.* Color, 20 min. (Tim Podell Productions, 1994).

www.carr.lib.md.us/authco/spinelli-j.htm

http://edupaperback.org/authorbios/spinell.html

Newbery Acceptance Speech: *Horn Book Magazine* 67(4):426 July/Aug 1991

Book Clip

They say Maniac Magee was born in a dump. They say his stomach was a cereal box and his heart a sofa spring. They say he kept an eight-inch cockroach on a leash and that rats stood guard over him while he slept. They say if you knew he was coming and you sprinkled salt on the ground and he ran over it, within two or three blocks he would be as slow as everybody else. They say. What's true, what's myth? It's hard to know. (page 1, hardback edition)

Do you want to know about Maniac Magee? Read the book to find out what's true and what's myth. Maybe it's all true?

Curriculum Connections

Literature (Legends, Creative Writing, Storytelling)

Spinelli writes "the history of a kid is one part fact, two parts legend, and three parts snowball." (page 2, hardback edition) What are the personal histories of students in your class? Do any of them have legendary status in any area, i.e., sports, academics, personal behavior, etc. Encourage students to tell or write their own legends, with embellishments, about their lives.

Refer to the following books for some familiar, and not-so-familiar, tall tales: *American Tall Tales* by Mary Pope Osborne (Knopf, 1992); Robert D. San Souci's *Larger Than Life: The Adventures of American Legendary Heroes* (Doubleday, 1991); *Cut from the Same Cloth: American Women of Myth, Legend and Tall Tale* by Robert D. San Souci (Philomel, 1993); *Swamp Angel* by Anne Issacs (Dutton, 1994); *John Henry* by Julius Lester (Dial Books for Young Readers, 1994); *The Bunyans* by Audrey Wood (Scholastic, 1996); and *How Georgie Radbourn Saved Baseball* by David Shannon (Scholastic, 1994).

Social Studies (Kid Power, Activism, Community)

While some students may not believe that just one boy, like Maniac, can have such a positive impact on his friends and community, there are countless examples of activism by kids. Kid Power is simply the remarkable influence students can have by their actions and volunteer efforts. Refer students to materials like *Kids with Courage: True Stories about Young People Making a Difference* by Barbara A. Lewis (Free Spirit, 1992); *It's Our World, Too! Stories of Young People Who Are Making a Difference* by Phillip Hoose (Joy Street, 1993); *The Kid's Guide to Service Projects: Over 500 Service Ideas for Young People Who Want to Make a Difference* by Barbara A. Lewis (Free Spirit, 1995); *Generation React: Activism for Beginners* by Danny Seo (Ballantine, 1997); *Heaven on Earth: 15-Minute Miracles to Change the World* by Danny Seo (Pocket, 1999); and *The Kid's Guide to Social Action: How to Solve the Social Problems You Choose—And Turn Creative Thinking into Positive Action* by Barbara A. Lewis (Free Spirit, 1998).

Related Websites

Peace Corps: Kids World – Make a Difference
   www.peacecorps.gov/kids/difference/

Youth Action Network
   www.mightymedia.com/act/

The Earth Day Groceries Project
   www.earthdaybags.org/

Social Issues (Homelessness, Picture Books for Older Readers, Research, Social Activism)

Maniac moves from place to place staying at homes of friends and living in the bandshell near the zoo. To launch discussions and further exploration of homelessness, use some of the excellent picture books for older readers such as *Fly Away Home* by Eve Bunting (Clarion, 1991); *Ophelia's Shadow Theatre* by Michael

Ende (Overlook Press, 1989); *This Home We Have Made, Esta Casa Que Hemos Hecho* by Anna Hammond and Joe Matunis (Crown, 1993); *Broken Umbrellas* by Kate Spohn (Viking, 1994); *Way Home* by Libby Hathorn (Crown, 1994); *Space Travellers* by Margaret Wild, (Scholastic, 1993); *We Are All in the Dumps with Jack and Guy: Two Nursery Rhymes with Pictures* illustrated by Maurice Sendak (HarperCollins, 1993); and *December* by Eve Bunting (Harcourt Brace, 1997).

Students can conduct research about the homeless (including those in your community) from reports in periodicals, newspapers, television, and online. Final projects might include suggestions for assisting the homeless, writing guest editorials for a local paper, interviewing local officials, volunteering at a soup kitchen, collecting mittens or other clothes, and/or arranging for schools to donate leftover cafeteria food to local shelters.

Related Websites

The National Coalition for the Homeless
  http://nch.ari.net/

Stand Up for Kids
  www.standupforkids.org/

Homelessness: Interdisciplinary Thematic Unit
  www.stark.k12.oh.us/DOCS/units/homeless/

Spotlight on Literature: Write a Letter to an Editor
  www.mmhschool.com/teach/reading/wl65a.html

Keep on Reading

Tangerine by Edward Bloor (Harcourt Brace, 1997). Even though Paul is practically blind he still is successful at playing soccer and making new friends—in spite of his disturbing older brother.

The Adventures of Blue Avenger by Norma Howe (Henry Holt, 1999). After his father's death, David changes his name to "Blue Avenger" and stumbles into a multitude of adventures.

Slot Machine by Chris Lynch (HarperCollins, 1995). The summer camp that fourteen-year-old Elvin is sent to is really a training ground for future athletes, however Elvin refuses to conform.

The Mouse Rap by Walter Dean Myers (HarperTrophy, 1992). Fourteen-year-old Mouse and his friends have an eventful summer searching for a treasure hidden in an abandoned building in Harlem.

Holes by Louis Sachar (Farrar, Straus & Giroux, 1998). Stanley Yelnats befriends an illiterate boy, saves him from injustice, finds a buried treasure, and breaks his family's curse.

Shots on a Goal by Rich Wallace (Knopf, 1997). Barry and Joey's close friendship is threatened by Joey's dominating behavior on and off the soccer field.

1991

HONOR

The True Confessions of Charlotte Doyle

Avi

Plot Summary

Thirteen-year-old Charlotte Doyle had eagerly anticipated her voyage across the ocean to rejoin her family. But when she finds herself the only passenger and female aboard the *Seahawk*, she senses trouble ahead. The captain seems to be charming and easily persuades Charlotte to be "eyes and ears among the men." When she realizes the captain isn't the gentleman he appears to be, Charlotte begins concealing information about an impending mutiny. To prove her loyalty to the crew, she passes a rigorous test (scaling the rigging to the masthead), and is accepted as a valuable member of the crew. The voyage becomes a struggle for survival as the captain becomes increasingly brutal and the ship sails into a hurricane.

Tips

The twists and turns of this suspenseful adventure will intrigue both boys and girls, despite a female protagonist, and the entire book provides a great read-aloud experience. However, to entice students to read on their own, read aloud part one (twelve chapters). Consider reproducing and enlarging the diagram of the ship (see the appendix) for a classroom display to enhance the read-aloud experience. Also provide *Stephen Biesty's Cross-Sections Man-of-War* by Stephen Biesty (DK, 1993), which features eighteenth-century British man-of-war ships bearing many similarities to Charlotte's ship *The Seahawk*.

Related Tips

"The Inside Story: The True Confessions of Charlotte Doyle" by Avi in *Book Links* (within *Booklist* 87(12):1225-1230 Feb 15, '91).

www.mcdougallittell.com/lit/litcon/true/guide.htm

Author Information

Born in New York in 1937, Avi (a nickname given to him by his twin sister) Wortis grew up in Brooklyn. As a child,

Just the Facts

LC 90-30624. 215p. 1990. $18.95 (ISBN 0-531-05893-X). Orchard Books/Watts.

Paperback. 1990. $4.99 (ISBN 0-380-71475-2). Avon.

Audio book. Unabridged, 6 hours. 1992. $39 (ISBN 1-556-90593-0). Recorded Books.

Genres: historical fiction, adventure

Themes: transatlantic voyages, sailing, revenge, friendship, danger, violence, evil, murder, racism, independence, courage, justice, self discovery, mutiny, tyrants, betrayal, loyalty, choices, hurricanes, gender roles

Readability: Sixth grade

Interest Level: Fifth through tenth grade

Review Citations:

Booklist 87(1):44 Sept 1, 1990

Bulletin of the Center for Children's Books 44(3):53 Nov 1990

English Journal 80(8):85 Dec 1991

Horn Book Magazine 67(1):65-6 Jan/Feb 1991

Publishers Weekly 237(37):128 Sept 14, 1990

School Library Journal 36(9):221+ Sept 1990

Wilson Library Bulletin 65(8):100 Apr 1991

Avi had trouble writing, spelling and punctuating. He suffered from a disorder known as dysgraphia, but his love for reading and the guidance of a tutor helped him overcome this difficulty. Avi graduated from Columbia University with a degree in library science. He began writing for children when his sons were small. Avi says he writes quickly … and slowly, with many rewrites. "What I always seek is a good, suspenseful story, rich in emotions, contradiction, irony—a story that grabs, makes you want to race to the end. At the same time I'm working hard to make the characters and ideas stay with the readers long after the last page." Avi acknowledges that his power as a writer comes from his "strength as a reader."

Avi was offered a television contract for a movie version of "Charlotte" but refused when the producers wanted to change the ending to make Charlotte remain with her family and change her father's mind. Refusing the offer, Avi told them "Sorry, you've got the wrong Charlotte." Researching material for the book involved spending large amounts of time in libraries and museums. Avi reports that he "read 30 to 40 books and lived with maritime maps all over the house."

Related Author Resources

Avi by Lois Markham (Learning Works, 1996)
www.avi-writer.com/
www.ipl.org/youth/AskAuthor/Avi.html
www.scils.rutgers.edu/special/kay/avi.html
http://falcon.jmu.edu/~ramseyil/avi.htm
http://tlc.ai.org/avi.htm

Book Clip

Not every thirteen-year-old girl is accused of murder, brought to trial, and found guilty. But I was just such a girl, and my story is worth relating even if it did happen years ago. Be warned, however, this is no Story of a Bad Boy, no What Katy Did. If strong ideas and action offend you, read no more. Find another companion to share your idle hours. For my part I intend to tell the truth as I lived it. But before I begin relating what happened, you must know something about me as I was in the year 1832—when these events transpired. At the time my name was Charlotte Doyle. And though I have kept the name, I am not—for reasons you will soon discover—the same Charlotte Doyle. (page 1, hardback edition)

This is the beginning of Charlotte Doyle's "true

confessions." Read on to find out just who the real Charlotte Doyle is.

Curriculum Connections

Art (Drawing, Painting, Sculpting)

Using Avi's vivid descriptions of the sailors, some students can sketch or paint their portraits. Exhibit the results in a "Gallery of the *Seahawk*." Include captions describing the crew members and their personal characteristics, utilizing quotations from the book to enhance descriptions. Encourage other students to replicate the ship (see appendix) and the bowsprit.

Related Websites

Ships to Quebec 1820
    www.dcs.uwaterloo.ca/~marj/genealogy/ships/ships 1820.html
Figureheads and Carvings
    www.mysticseaport.org/public/collections/curatorial/ carvings.curatorial.html

Creative Dramatics (Writing, Government, Trials--Mock)

Student(s) can write a script of the shipboard trial featured in chapter 18. Cast the characters and reenact the drama as a mock trial. Mock trials should include a judge, defense team, prosecution team, witnesses, selection of a fair jury, and the accused. Other stories that can be adapted into mock trials include the witch trial in Sid Fleischman's *The 13th Floor: A Ghost Story* (Greenwillow, 1997); Eugene Triviza's *The Three Little Wolves and the Big Bad Pig* (Macmillan, 1993); Jon Scieszka's *The True Story of the 3 Little Pigs by A. Wolf* (Viking Kestrel, 1989). Useful implementation ideas for Scieszka's book are available in "The Wolf on Trial" in *School Library Journal* 39(9):166 Sept 1993.

Related Websites

Taking the Courthouse to the Schoolroom
    www.rain.org/courthouse/order.htm
Washington State Courts: Education
    www.wa.gov/courts/educate/home.htm

History (Sea Voyages, Ships, Trade)

Research the history of ships, sea voyages and trade that took place during the eighteenth and nineteenth centuries. Provide books such as *Famous Ships: A Quick History of Ships with 8 Authentic Models to Make and Display* by Leon Baxter (Ideals Children's Books, 1993); *Stephen Biesty's Cross-Sections Man-of-War* by Richard Platt (DK, 1993); *The Sailor's*

Alphabet by Michael McCurdy (Houghton Mifflin, 1998); *Tall Ships of the World* by C. Keith Wilbur (Chelsea House, 1997); *Boat* by Eric Kentley (Knopf, 1992); and *The World of the Pirate* by Val Garwood, (Peter Bedrick, 1997).

Related Websites

1828 Voyage
   www.dcs.uwaterloo.ca/~marj/genealogy/eye1820s.html

Keep on Reading

Hurricane, Open Seas, 1844 by Kathleen Duey (Aladdin, 1999). The captain's daughter, Rebecca Whittier, and John Lowe, an indentured servant, save the ship's cargo after a horrendous storm.

The Wreckers by Iain Lawrence (Delacorte, 1998). Lured onto a rocky coast during a storm at sea, John enlists the help of Simon Mawgan and his niece, Mary, in order to rescue his imprisoned father.

The Pirate's Son by Geraldine McCaughrean (Scholastic, 1998). Nathan and his sister Maud are taken aboard a pirate ship and learn about a vastly different life.

Grace by Jill Paton Walsh (Sunburst, 1994). A lighthouse keeper's daughter, Grace Darling and her father heroically rescue nine shipwreck victims.

Jo and the Bandit by Willo Davis Roberts (Atheneum, 1992). Twelve-year-old Jo is on her way west to stay with her uncle when her stagecoach is robbed.

Jackaroo by Cynthia Voigt (Macmillan, 1985). Gwyn takes on the persona of the legendary outlaw, Jackaroo.

1992

MEDAL

Shiloh

Phyllis Reynolds Naylor

Plot Summary

Eleven-year-old Marty rescues a mistreated dog and discovers the joys and sorrows of keeping a secret pet. He becomes tangled in a web of lies while becoming more and more attached to the dog he names Shiloh. When the family learns his secret, Marty's father insists they return the dog even though he knows Shiloh will be abused again by his cruel owner. It's hard for Marty to come to grips with the fine line between what is right and what is wrong.

Tips

Encourage students to read this on their own because dialect is difficult for most people to read aloud. However, consider reading aloud the first five chapters (or using the audio version) to hook readers on worrying about Shiloh's fate. All dog lovers will be attracted to this book. Sequels, both published by Atheneum, are *Shiloh Season* (1996) and *Saving Shiloh* (1997). Two films, *Shiloh* (1997) and *Shiloh 2: Shiloh Season* (1999) are available on videotape.

Related Tips

Shiloh by Phyllis Reynolds Naylor (Scholastic, 1997).
www.simonsays.com/kids/teachers/teacher_guide.cfm
www.randomhouse.com/teachers/guides/shil.html
www.umcs.maine.edu/~orono/collaborative/shiloh.html

Author Information

Born in Indiana in 1933, Phyllis R. Naylor was raised in the Midwest by a reading family. Even though she never wanted to admit it, her parents read aloud to her until she was in her teens. Naylor sold her first short story for $4.67 when she was sixteen. She has been writing ever since, enabling her to pay her college expenses. Naylor writes alternately for children and adults, turning out both nonfiction and fiction in numerous genres. Married to a speech pathologist and mother to two children, Naylor enjoys traveling, beach-combing, singing sixteenth-century madrigals, and playing the dulcimer. However, writing is her favorite activity and she isn't happy unless she spends time everyday writing.

Many of Naylor's books are based on personal

Just the Facts

LC 90-603. 144p. 1991. $15 (ISBN 0-689-31614-3). Atheneum.

Paperback. $5.50 (ISBN 0-440-40752-4). Dell/Yearling.

Audio book. Abridged, 3 hours. 1992. $15.99 (ISBN 0-553-47116-3). Bantam Doubleday Dell Audio.

Audio book. *The Phyllis Reynolds Naylor Value Collection : Shiloh, Saving Shiloh, Shiloh Season.* Unabridged. 1999. $24.95 (ISBN 0-553-52633-2). Bantam Books Audio.

Genre: contemporary realistic fiction

Themes: dogs, values, ethics, courage, animal cruelty, pets, problem solving, love, Appalachian life, lies, friendship,

kindness, loyalty, determination, responsibility, secrecy, family life, rural life

Readability: Fourth grade

Interest Level: Fourth through eighth grade

Review Citations:

Booklist 88(7):696 Dec 1, 1991

Bulletin of the Center for Children's Books 45(2):45 Oct 1991

Horn Book Magazine 68(1):74-75 Jan/Feb 1992

School Library Journal 37(9):258 Sept 1991

experiences and *Shiloh* is no exception. While Naylor and her husband were visiting friends in West Virginia and out for a walk, they encountered a stray beagle and Naylor made the mistake of whistling to it. The dog followed them to their friend's house and stayed outside all day in the rain waiting for someone to come out. Naylor came face to face with the issue of abandoned pets and her method of dealing with this heartrending problem was to write a book.

Related Author Resources

How I Came to Be a Writer by Phyllis Reynolds Naylor (Aladdin, 1987).

Video: *Good Conversation! A Talk with Phyllis Reynolds Naylor.* Color, 26 min. (Tim Podell Productions, 1991).

www.randomhouse.com/teachers/guides/nayl.html

www.ipl.org/youth/AskAuthor/Naylor.html

Newbery Acceptance Speech: *Horn Book Magazine* 68(4):404+ July/Aug 1992.

Book Clip

While out for a walk in the West Virginia mountains, eleven-year-old Marty finds a stray dog. Or maybe the dog finds him.

> I figure that's the last I'll see of the beagle, and I get halfway down the road again before I look back. There he is. I stop. He stops. I go. He goes. And then, hardly thinking on it, I whistle. It's like pressing a magic button. The beagle comes barreling toward me, legs going lickety-split, long ears flopping, tail sticking up like a flagpole. This time, when I put out my hand, he licks all my fingers and jumps up against my leg, making little yelps in his throat. He can't get enough of me, like I'd been saying no all along and now I'd said yes, he could come. (page 15, hardback and paperback editions)

This beagle belongs to someone but seems eager to be Marty's pal. Marty names him Shiloh and he becomes more than a friend.

Curriculum Connections

Sports (Hunting, Hunter Safety, Laws, Mathematics)

Judd is not a good sportsman and illegally poaches and hunts out-of-season. Invite a representative from the Fish and Game Department to discuss hunting laws, gun safety practices, and other issues. Find out about hunter

safety classes in your area. Collect national and state statistics on hunting accidents and law infringements to use for information and comparisons. Consult *The Field & Stream Firearms Safety Handbook* by Doug Hunting Painter (Lyons , 1999); *A Family Goes Hunting* by Dorothy Hinshaw Patent (Clarion, 1991); and other materials for more information.

Related Websites

USA & Canada Hunting Casualty Stats and Reports
    www.dfg.ca.gov/ihea/accident.html

International Hunter Education Association
    www.ihea.com/index.shtml

Firearms and Hunting Safety Rules
    www.safenebraska.org/SafetyInfo/HuntingNFirearms.html

Science (Dog Obedience, Behavior, Training)

Students can learn the basics of dog obedience training and the underlying behavior of dogs by consulting the following *Dogwatching* by Desmond Morris (Crown, 1993); *Dog Obedience Training: A Complete and Up-to-Date Guide* by Ross Allan (Chelsea House, 1997); *Dog Training for Kids* by Carol Lea Benjamin (Howell, 1988); *Understanding Man's Best Friend: Why Dogs Look and Act the Way They Do* by Ann Squire (Macmillan, 1991); *Teach Your Dog to Behave: Simple Solutions to Over 300 Common Dog Behavior Problems from A to Z* by Batiks Dibra and Elizabeth Randolph (Signet, 1994); and *The Complete Idiot's Guide to Fun and Tricks with Your Dog* by Sarah Hodgson (Macmillan, 1997).

Related Websites

Collar & Lead Dog Obedience Training Page
    www.users.bigpond.com/winron/

Training Your Dog
    www.trainingyourdog.com/

Ethics (Morality, Values, Dilemmas)

This short novel is an ideal springboard for discussions of issues concerning moral dilemmas such as the gray areas of right and wrong, breaking the law for the greater good, lying, stealing, etc. Compare and contrast *Shiloh* with novels with similar themes like *The Giver* by Lois Lowry (Houghton Mifflin, 1993); *On My Honor* by Marion Bauer (Houghton Mifflin, 1987); *One-Eyed Cat* by Paula Fox (Yearling, 1985); *Weasel* by Cynthia DeFelice (Macmillan, 1990); *Hoops* by Walter Dean Myers (Laurel Leaf, 1983); *Camouflage* by Gloria D. Miklowitz (Harcourt Brace, 1998); and *Poor Badger* by

K. M. Peyton (Delacorte, 1992).

Keep on Reading

Strider by Beverly Cleary (William Morrow, 1991). Fourteen-year-old Leigh finds an abandoned dog on the beach and agrees to share ownership of the dog with his best friend Barry.

Jim Ugly by Sid Fleischman (Greenwillow, 1992). Jake has nobody but a mongrel wolf dog named Jim Ugly, and together they take off to look for his missing father.

Look Back, Moss by Betty Levin (Greenwillow, 1998). Jody develops a special bond with Moss, an injured dog his mother brings home to heal.

Wander by Susan Hart Lindquist (Delacorte, 1998). After their mother dies, twelve-year-old James and his younger sister meet Wander, a stray dog who needs protection.

Not My Dog by Colby Rodowsky (Farrar, Straus & Giroux, 1999). After Ellie turns nine, she's allowed to have a puppy but she didn't expect to have to take her aunt's full-grown dog named Preston.

The Junkyard Dog by Erika Tamar (Knopf, 1997). Katie convinces her stepfather to let her feed the mistreated junkyard dog she passes every day on her way home from school.

1992

HONOR

Nothing but the Truth
A Documentary Novel
Avi

Plot Summary

Ninth grader Philip Malloy's failing grade in Miss Narwin's English class triggers a series of events that rapidly head out of control. To annoy her, Philip hums along with the daily tape of the "Star Spangled Banner" which is played in every homeroom. When he is suspended for disrupting Miss Narwin's homeroom, Philip tells his parents he has been punished for singing the national anthem. The situation escalates as school board members, local politicians, national news reporters, and talk radio show hosts become involved.

Tips

The book's unusual format allows readers to eavesdrop and peruse numerous diary entries, letters, memos, and conversations and will appeal to most, including reluctant readers. It is perfect for an entire class to read and discuss. Classroom sets would be especially useful in classes dealing with ethics, values, and issues and in U.S. Government classes.

Related Tips

"Book Strategies: Nothing but the Truth: A Documentary Novel by Avi" *Book Links* 1(3): 60-61 Jan. 1992.

www.umcs.maine.edu/~orono/collaborative/nothing.html

www.mcdougallittell.com/lit/litcon/nothing/guide.htm

Author Information

Born in New York in 1937, Avi (a nickname given to him by his twin sister) Wortis grew up in Brooklyn. As a child, Avi had trouble writing, spelling and punctuating. He suffered from a disorder known as dysgraphia, but his love for reading and the guidance of a tutor helped him overcome this difficulty. Avi graduated from Columbia University with a degree in library science. He began writing for children when his sons were small. Avi says he writes quickly … and slowly, with many rewrites. "What I always seek is a good, suspenseful story, rich in emotions, contradiction, irony—a story that grabs, makes you want to race to the end. At the same time I'm

Just the Facts

LC 91-9200. 192p. 1991. $14.95 (ISBN 0-531-05959-6). Orchard Books.

Paperback. 212p. 1993. $4.99 (ISBN 0-380-71907-X). Avon Flare.

Genre: contemporary realistic fiction

Themes: ethics, school life, teachers, individual rights, insubordination, truth, suspension, communication, freedom of speech, patriotism, responsibility, media, politicians, diaries, rules, grades, sports--track, parents

Readability: Sixth grade

Interest Level: Seventh through twelfth grade

Review Citations:

Booklist 88(2):136 Sept 15, 1991

Bulletin of the Center for Children's Books 45(1):2 Sept 1991

English Journal 81(7):91 Nov 1992

Horn Book Magazine 68(1):78 Jan/Feb 1992

Publishers Weekly 238(40):105 Sept 5, 1991

School Library Journal 37(9):277 Sept 1991

Wilson Library Bulletin 66(4):101 Dec 1991

working hard to make the characters and ideas stay with the readers long after the last page." Avi acknowledges that his power as a writer comes from his "strength as a reader."

The structure behind *Nothing but the Truth* came from a 1930s form of theater called "Living Newspapers." These were dramatizations of problems and issues in American society presented through readings of documents as well as dialogue between actors.

Related Author Resources

Avi by Lois Markham (Learning Works, 1996)

www.avi-writer.com/

www.ipl.org/youth/AskAuthor/Avi.html

www.scils.rutgers.edu/special/kay/avi.html

http://falcon.jmu.edu/~ramseyil/avi.htm

http://tlc.ai.org/avi.htm

Book Clip

(Prop: create the memo on page 74, hardback edition.)

TO: Dr. Gertrude Doane, Principal

FROM: Dr. Joseph Palleni, Assistant Principal...

Philip Malloy (ninth grade) has been suspended for two days—effective today—for causing a disturbance in Miss Narwin's homeroom class. Because I feel that the problem may have arisen out of some obscure tension between teacher and student, I decided it was advisable to transfer the boy to Mr. Lunser's homeroom. Since I assume nothing more will come of this, I'm not aware of anything that requires your further attention. (page 74, hardback edition)

Boy, was the assistant principal wrong in believing this event is over. The anger Philip has for Miss Narwin, and the manner in which he explains what happened to his parents propels this event to the attention of the nation. What is the truth in *Nothing but the Truth*?

Curriculum Connections

Creative Dramatics (Theater, Living Newspapers, History, 1930s, Great Depression)

Nothing but the Truth is well suited for dramatization. The structure behind the story comes from a 1930s form of theater called "Living Newspapers." These dramatizations featured problems and issues in American society

presented through readings of documents as well as dialogue between actors. Find out more about the Living Newspapers theatre productions in *Liberty Deferred, And Other Living Newspapers of the 1930s Federal Theatre Project* edited by Lorraine Brown (George Mason University Press, 1989).

Present *Nothing but the Truth* as a play with students assuming the roles of Philip, Miss Narwin, the principal, the news reporter, etc. Videotape the finished product and view for discussion starters in your classroom or others. Add the finished videotape to your school and/or public library collection.

Related Websites

National Archives and Records Administration: Work Pays America
 www.nara.gov/exhall/newdeal/work1.html

The Federal Theatre Page: Subversive Theatre
 www.dc.net/stanley/dies.html

Journalism (Ethics, Truth, Newspapers, Perspective)

Readers of *Nothing but the Truth* will easily realize that a news report on television or in the newspaper may not be absolutely true. Use this as an opportunity to scrutinize local and national journalism. Invite students to look at contemporary news stories in your local newspaper and ask them to consider other perspectives beyond what is written. What is the complete truth?

Go on to explore the ethics of journalists and journalism. Interested students can learn more by reading the yearly winners of the *Best Newspaper Writing: Winners— The American Society of Newspaper Editors Competition* (Bonus Books); *Slick Spins and Fractured Facts: How Cultural Myths Distort the News* by Caryl Rivers (Columbia University Press, 1996); *What Are Journalists For?* by Jay Rosen (Yale University Press, 1999); *Media Wizards: A Behind-the-Scenes Look at Media Manipulations* by Catherine Gourley (Twenty-First Century, 1999); and *News Values: Ideas for an Information Age* by Jack Fuller (University of Chicago Press, 1996).

Related Websites

The Ethics of Civic Journalism: Independence as the Guide
 www.poynter.org/research/me/me_civic.htm

Columbia Journalism Review
 www.cjr.org/

Society of Professional Journalists: Ethics in Journalism
 http://spj.org/ethics/index.htm

Speech (Communication, Telecommunication, Media Literacy, Current Events, Talk Shows)

The events in *Nothing but the Truth* capture the attention of everyone … and everyone is talking. What do people talk about in your school? Listen for phrases like "They said …," "I heard …," etc. Consider how these phrases relate to the childhood gossip game "Telephone" and use this as an opportunity to develop important media literacy skills in your students. Teach students how to evaluate media messages critically.

Students can explore media literacy with regard to radio and television talk shows, network and public television and radio stations, public access cable channels, and the Internet. Invite guests and start a dialogue about communication. Some students might be interested in hosting a talk show (check your public access cable channels) that focuses on school, local, national, and/or international issues.

Related Websites

Media Literacy — What Is It and Why Teach It?
www.media-awareness.ca/eng/med/bigpict/what.htm

Center for Media Literacy
www.medialit.org/

Educational Resources in Media Literacy/Studies
www.cln.org/subjects/media.html

Keep on Reading

Painting the Black by Carl Deuker (Houghton, 1997). Ryan faces a moral dilemma when he alone knows that Josh is responsible for a sexual attack on a classmate.

The Day They Came to Arrest the Book by Nat Hentoff (Dell, 1983). Barney battles censorship when *The Adventures of Huckleberry Finn* is removed from the school library.

T-Backs, T-Shirts, Coat, and Suit by E.L. Konigsburg (Atheneum, 1993). Freedom of expression and freedom from conformity are issues for Aunt Bernadette and Chloë.

Spite Fences by Trudy Krisher (Bantam Doubleday Dell, 1996). From behind her camera lens, Maggie discovers bigotry and cruelty in her community.

Monster by Walter Dean Myers (HarperCollins, 1999). A fourteen-year-old boy is on trial and maintains courage by writing a movie screenplay of his experiences as they happen.

The Wave by Todd Strasser and Morton Rhue (Laurel-Leaf, 1981). Based on a true incident in a history class, group pressure creates a Nazi environment.

1992

HONOR

The Wright Brothers
How They Invented the Airplane
Russell Freedman

Plot Summary

Orville and Wilbur Wright's attempts to create and fly the first airplane are chronicled using their own original photographs in addition to archival photographs, excerpts from letters and journals, diagrams, and narrative.

Tips

Read aloud chapter one (two pages) to introduce Freedman's compelling story of, what some consider, the most important invention of the twentieth century. The book consists of ten chapters with additional sections about the photographs, a list of places to visit, a bibliography, and an index. For a different approach, consider reading the picture book *Our Neighbor Is a Strange, Strange Man* by Tres Seymour (Orchard, 1999) followed by the Book Clip.

Related Tips

"The Inside Story: Russell Freedman's The Wright Brothers" *Book Links* 1(5):28-30 May 1992
www.umcs.maine.edu/~orono/collaborative/wright.html

Author Information

Russell Freedman was born in 1929 in San Francisco and graduated from the University of California - Berkeley with a major in English. After being drafted, Freedman spent two years in Korea and then began working for the Associated Press. Later he wrote television publicity for an ad agency but entertained "vague yearnings" to write books. He was inspired to write a biography of Louis Braille and his career as a writer of nonfiction for young people began.

Freedman does all his own research and becomes thoroughly immersed in the subject. One thousand pages of research may only yield ten pages of text. He stayed in Orville Wright's mansion while researching this book, slept in his room and showered in his inventive bathroom for inspiration.

Just the Facts

LC 90-48440. 128p. 1991. $16.95 (ISBN 0-8234-875-2). Holiday House.
Paperback. 1994. $12.95 (ISBN 0-823-41082-X). Holiday House.
Video. 40 min. 1992. (ISBN 0-383-05171-1). American School Publishers.
Genres: nonfiction, biography
Themes: Orville Wright (1871–1948), Wilbur Wright (1867–1912), aeronautics, aviation history, flight, airplanes, inventions, brothers, technology, photography, printing, bicycles, kites, hang gliders, problem solving

Readability: Seventh grade
Interest Level: Fourth through tenth grade
Review Citations:
Booklist 95(7):680 Dec 1, 1998
Bulletin of the Center for Childrens Books 44(10):236 June 1991
Horn Book Magazine 67(4):475 July 1991
New Yorker 67(40)148 Nov 25, 1991
Publishers Weekly 238(20):73 May 3, 1991
School Library Journal 37(6):116 June 1991

Related Author Resources

www.indiana.edu/~eric_rec/ieo/bibs/freedman.html

Book Clip

On December 8, 1903, an early flight attempt of the *Great Aerodrome* resulted in the near death of the pilot who sank into an icy river. His frozen clothes had to be cut off his body to save him. Newspapers had a field day.

> *The New York Times* commented that a man-carrying airplane would eventually be built—but only if mathematicians and engineers worked steadily for the next one million to ten million years. It didn't take that long at all. Exactly nine days after Langley's *Great Aerodrome* sank in the Potomac, Orville Wright took off on history's first successful airplane flight. (page 23, hardback and paperback editions)

Curriculum Connections

History (Flight, Mythology, Timelines)

Students can create a timeline depicting the chronological history of airplane development beginning with Icarus' flight with artificial wings to the present. Include the inventors and dates Freedman mentioned in chapter three—a Benedictine monk named Eilmer, Leonardo da Vinci, Sir George Cayley, Otto Lilienthal, Samuel Pierpoint Langley, and Octave Chanute. A helpful resource is *Before the Wright Brothers* by Don Berliner (Lerner, 1990).

Related Websites

FirstFlight: The Wright Brothers
  http://firstflight.open.ac.uk/

National Air and Space Museum: Exhibitions
  www.nasm.edu/nasm/NASMexh.html

Science Museum London: History of Flight- Frost Ornithopter
  www.nmsi.ac.uk/on-line/flight/flight/frost.htm

Lesson Level 1 - Objectives for History of Flight
  www.allstar.fiu.edu/aero/obj1hist.htm

History (Wright Brothers, Research, Photography, Internet, Newspapers, Bibliographies)

Students can find out more about the Wright brothers by further exploring and using the research data listed by Freedman. Consult the photographic information preceding the table of contents and "About the Photographs" (pages 118–120), "Places to Visit" (pages 121–122), and "For Further Reading" (pages 123–124).

Using newspaper archives, historical photographs, and related books available in local libraries and through inter-library loan, students will learn more about the Wright brothers and their inventions. Be sure to search local newspaper archives for coverage of the events as they happened and citizens' reactions to those first flights.

Related Websites

The Wright Stuff
  www.pbs.org/wgbh/pages/amex/wright/

Henry Ford Museum & Greenfield Village: The Wright Brothers
  www.hfmgv.org/histories/wright/wrights.html

Library of Congress: American Memory – Collection Finder
  http://memory.loc.gov/ammem/collections/finder.html

History (Inventions, Writing, Speech, Debate, Research)

As citizens of the twenty-first century, today's students can examine inventions in the previous century from a historical perspective. What do students think was the most important invention of the twentieth century? Books like *Fantastic Millennium Facts* by Russell Ash (DK, 1999) and *Children's History of the 20th Century* (DK, 1999) will be useful for considering possibilities like the airplane, personal computers, television, the Internet, telephones, penicillin, plastic, etc. Students should select a topic, research its impact on the world, and present their findings. An additional activity is having those who select the same topic form debate teams and defend their choice.

Related Websites

20th Century Inventions: From Mind to Matter—Timeline
  http://library.advanced.org/21798/data/tqmainsite/timeline/

The 20th Century
  http://cnn.com/SPECIALS/1999/century/

Computer, TV and Refrigerator Top Technologies of 20th Century, Public Survey Shows
  www.harris.com/harris/whats_new/survey-20th-century.html

Jerome and Dorothy Lemelson Center for the Study of Invention and Innovation
  www.si.edu/lemelson/

Keep on Reading

The U.S. Space Camp Book of Astronauts by Anne Baird (William Morrow, 1996). Biographical profiles of fourteen astronauts are highlighted with numerous photographs.

An American Hero: The True Story of Charles A. Lindbergh by Barry Denenberg (Scholastic, 1996). A biography of this famous aviator uses excerpts from his own writing along with photographs, charts, and maps.

Visions of a Flying Machine: The Wright Brothers and the Process of Invention by Peter L. Jakab (Smithsonian Institution, 1997). This is a detailed accounting of the Wright brothers' preparation for the historic 1903 flight.

Red-Tail Angels: The Story of the Tuskegee Airmen of World War II by Patricia McKissack (Walker, 1995). This history of African American aviation pioneers blends narrative with photographs and a bibliography.

Flying Machine by Andrew Nahum (Knopf, 1990). The history and development of aircraft is traced through photographs and brief narratives.

Sky Pioneer: A Photobiography of Amelia Earhart by Corrine Szabo (National Geographic Society, 1997). With photographs and narrative, Amelia Earhart's flight career is celebrated.

1993

MEDAL

Missing May

Cynthia Rylant

Plot Summary

An orphan, six-year-old Summer is lovingly adopted by her elderly Uncle Ob and Aunt May. Six years later, May dies leaving Summer and Uncle Ob to cope with her death and their grief. Cletus Underwood, another of the unusual characters, befriends Summer and Ob, and eventually helps them focus on good memories and the future.

Tips

The twelve chapters are divided into two parts. Reading aloud the first section (through page 43, paperback edition) will expose students to a beautifully written vignette and, perhaps, inspire them to finish the book on their own. Thoughtful readers will appreciate Rylant's serious topic and concise writing.

Related Tips

www.umcs.maine.edu/~orono/collaborative/missing.html

www.westga.edu/~kidreach/missingmay.html

www.carolhurst.com/subjects/appalachia.html

http://eduscapes.com/newbery/93a.html

Author Information

Cynthia Rylant is a prolific writer of award-winning books for the picture book set as well as for older readers. Her own childhood memories and experiences are recalled in much of her work. An imaginative child, Rylant grew up in the rustic West Virginia mountains, raised primarily by her grandparents. A college English class turned Rylant on to writers and literature but she didn't begin writing until after she began working in the children's room of a public library and grew to love children's books. Her writing reflects the joys and sorrows of her own childhood. Rylant now lives a fairly reclusive life in western Oregon.

Related Author Resources

Best Wishes by Cynthia Rylant (Richard C. Owen, 1992)

But I'll Be Back Again by Cynthia Rylant (Beech Tree, 1993)

Just the Facts

LC 91-23303. 89p. 1992. $14.95 (ISBN 0-531-08596-1). Orchard Books.

Paperback. 96p. 1993. $4.99 (ISBN 0-440-40865-2). Dell.

Audio book. 2 hours. 1996. $16.99 (ISBN 0-553-47445-6). Bantam Doubleday Dell Audio.

Audio book. 2 hours. 1996. $19 (ISBN 0-788-70377-3). Recorded Books.

Genre: contemporary realistic fiction

Themes: love, death, spirit, orphans, home, adoption, grief, friendship, whirligigs, spiritualism, country life, depression, memories, quests, near death experiences, West Virginia

Readability: Fifth grade

Interest Level: Sixth through tenth grade

Review Citations:

Book Report 11(2):52 Sept/Oct 1992

Booklist 88(12):1105 Feb 15, 1992

Bulletin of the Center for Childrens Books 45(9):192 Mar 1992

English Journal 82(8):73 Dec 1993

Horn Book Magazine 68(2):206 Mar 1992

Publishers Weekly 239(7):82 Feb 3, 1992

School Library Journal 38(3):241 Mar 1992

Wilson Library Bulletin 66(10):122 June 1992

"Rylant: Growing Up in Appalachia" *Book Links.* page 15, May 1991

"Appalachia through the Eyes of Rylant and Houston" *Book Links* 5(5):36 May 1996

Video: *Meet the Picture Book Author: Cynthia Rylant.* Color, 10 min. (Miller-Brody, 1990).

http://falcon.jmu.edu/~ramseyil/rylant.htm

www.tetranet.net/users/stolbert/research/rylant.html# contents 5/96, p.36

Newbery Acceptance Speech: *Horn Book Magazine* 69(4):416 Jul/Aug 1993

Book Clip

After Aunt May and Uncle Ob adopted Summer they had a wonderful life together. For the first time in her young life, Summer has been truly loved and happy. May took care of them both and kept them all strong. But after May dies …

> … we're not strong anymore. And I think Ob's going to die, truly die, if I can't figure a way to mend his sorry broken heart. And if Ob does go, goes off to be with May, then it'll be just me …. (page 16, paperback edition)

Summer's survival depends on finding a way to help Ob cope with *Missing May.*

Curriculum Connections

Art (Folk Art, Carving, Whirligies)

Uncle Ob's hobby is creating an unusual series of whirligigs (page 6, paperback edition) entitled "The Mysteries." They include Thunderstorm, Heaven, Fire, Love, Dreams, Death, as well as a representation of his wife, May. Ob's whirligigs were more abstract than traditional animals, scenes, etc. Students who have whirligigs can bring them to share prior to a class project where all students make them as an art activity. Provide guides like *Whirligigs & Weathervanes: A Celebration of Wind Gadgets with Dozens of Creative Projects to Make* by David Schoonmaker (Lark Books, 1992); *Wind Toys That Spin, Sing, Twirl & Whirl* by Cindy Burda (Sterling, 1999); and *Foxfire 10: Railroad Lore, Boardinghouses, Depression-Era Appalachia, Chair Making, Whirligigs, Snake Canes, and Gourd Art* edited by George P. Reynolds and Susan Walker (Anchor, 1993). In addition, Paul Fleischman's young adult novel *Whirligig* (Henry Holt, 1998) will similarly appeal to some readers.

Related Websites

From Windmills to Whirligigs: A Conversation With Vollis Simpson
   www.smm.org/sln/vollis/video.htm

Try These: Whirligigs
   www.smm.org/sln/vollis/trythese/trythese.html

Psychology (Near Death Experiences, Spirituality)

Cletus is fascinated by near-death experiences and he is not alone. Newspaper accounts and television coverage of people who have had near death experiences have captured the interest of many people. Students may be interested in knowing more. The following materials provide more information about this phenomenon: *Near-Death Experiences* by Elaine Landau (Millbrook, 1995) and *Beyond the Light: The Mysteries and Revelations of Near Death Experiences* by P. M. H. Atwater (Avon, 1997).

Related Websites

Near Death Experiences
   http://ucl.broward.cc.fl.us/pathfinders%5cneardeath.htm

International Association for Near-Death Studies
   www.iands.org/

Science (Gardens, Plants, Community Gardens)

May's garden helped provide food for the family for the entire year, and it was an important and meaningful activity for her. Even if students don't live in rural areas, they can still become active gardeners—perhaps in a community garden setting. Use the following resources for interested students: *Down to Earth: Garden Secrets! Garden Stories! Garden Projects You Can Do!* created by Michael J. Rosen (Harcourt Brace, 1998); *The City Gardener's Cookbook: Totally Fresh, Mostly Vegetarian, Decidedly Delicious Recipes from Seattle's P-Patches* by Seattle's P-Patches and edited by N. Allen and D. Pierce (Sasquatch, 1997); *Seedfolks* by Paul Fleischman (HarperCollins, 1997); and *A Place to Grow: Voices and Images of Urban Gardeners* edited by David Hassler and Lynn Gregor (Pilgrim, 1999).

Related Websites

American Community Gardening Association
   www.communitygarden.org/

Urban Community Gardens
   http://alexia.lis.uiuc.edu/~sewells/communitygardens.htm

Keep on Reading

Chasing Redbird by Sharon Creech (HarperCollins, 1997). Clearing a historic trail gives Zinny the opportunity to deal with her aunt's recent death.

Walk Two Moons by Sharon Creech (HarperCollins, 1994). It takes a while, but eventually Sal comes to terms with her mother's desertion and death.

Words of Stone by Kevin Henkes (Greenwillow, 1992). Blaze's summer is spent dealing with his mother's death and befriending the angry girl who lives nearby.

Mick Harte Was Here by Barbara Park (Knopf, 1995). Devastated by the fatal bicycle accident of her brother Mick, Phoebe remembers his terrific sense of humor and funny pranks.

Flip-Flop Girl by Katherine Paterson (Dutton, 1994). Vinnie is struggling with a multitude of problems—the death of her father, her younger brother is mute with grief, and her only friend has a mysterious home life.

Belle Prater's Boy by Ruth White (Farrar, Straus & Giroux, 1996). Gypsy and Woodrow become fast friends as they help each other deal with grief and secrets.

1993

HONOR

What Hearts

Bruce Brooks

Plot Summary

Six-year-old Asa's life is abruptly altered when his mother divorces his father and remarries. His demanding stepfather and depressed mother force Asa to become independent and sort out the difficult family dynamics. Their frequent moves cause Asa to struggle with constantly making new friends and adjusting to different school situations and rules.

Tips

The four sections of this book, comprised of several chapters each, focus on the different ages and stages of Asa's life. Told in third person, this introspective and serious story will appeal to a likewise student.

Related Tips

www.umcs.maine.edu/~orono/collaborative/hearts. html

Author Information

Bruce Brooks has worked as a printer, magazine and newspaper reporter, and teacher, as well as an author of nonfiction and fiction for children. His novels relate significantly to events of his own childhood. Brooks' parents divorced when he was young, and he spent his childhood growing up in two households with two different lifestyles. He moved constantly and says this helped him overcome his shyness and become a good storyteller. Making new friends in new surroundings honed his observation skills, giving him fodder for characters and stories.

Related Author Resources

www.scils.rutgers.edu/special/kay/brooks.html

www.indiana.edu/~eric_rec/ieo/bibs/brooks.html

Book Clip

It's always difficult for stepparents and children to learn to get along. However, when one or the other is unwilling to compromise, it can be even worse.

> During their first couple of years as fake father and fake son, Dave had tried to make Asa do many things—but he was terrible at it, like a bulldog sergeant major crushing the recruit in a bad army movie. (page 100, hardback edition; page 105, paperback edition)

Just the Facts

LC 92-5305. 194p. 1992. $14.95 (ISBN 0-06-0211311-8). HarperCollins.

Paperback. 1995. $5.95 (ISBN 0-06-447127-6) HarperTrophy.

Audio book. Unabridged, 4.75 hours. 1997. (ISBN 0-788-70737-X). Recorded Books.

Genre: contemporary realistic fiction

Themes: divorce, families, remarriage, stepfathers, mothers and sons, moving, love, forgiveness, anger, friendship, school life, imagination, compassion, baseball, comics, poetry, depression, sports, suicide, jealousy

Readability: Fifth grade

Interest Level: Fifth through eighth grade

Review Citations:

Booklist 89(1):53 Sep 1, 1992

Bulletin of the Center for Childrens Books 46(4):106 Dec 1992

Horn Book Magazine 69(1):89 Jan 1993

Publishers Weekly 239(50):65 Nov 15, 1992

School Library Journal 38(11):116 Nov 1992

Wilson Library Bulletin 67(10):102 June 1993

Will the small battles that constantly occur between Asa and his stepfather end up in a full-fledged war? Whose heart will be broken?

Curriculum Connections

Language Arts (Poetry, Recitations, Multiple Voices, Choral Readings)

Although he preferred to perform solo, Asa is required to develop a poetry reading with another student. The teacher could have provided her students with a variety of poetry specifically designed for multiple voices. Create a classroom library with the following materials and stage your own poetry program: *Joyful Noise: Poems for Two Voices* (HarperCollins, 1998) and *I Am Phoenix: Poems for Two Voices* (HarperTrophy, 1989) by Paul Fleischman; and *Math Talk: Mathematical Ideas in Poems for Two Voices* by Theoni Pappas (Wide World, 1991).

Related Websites

Shared Voices in Poetry
   www.houstonisd.org/ImpactII/Winners/NARRATIVES/Teague.htm

Choral Speaking and Readers Theatre
   www.loiswalker.com/choralsp.html

Aaron Shepard's Reader's Theater Editions
   www.aaronshep.com/rt/RTE.html

Language Arts (Poetry, Narrative Poetry, Music, Picture Books for Older Readers)

Asa loves long, emotional narrative poems and your students may as well. Fortunately many ballads and narrative poems have been illustrated and published in picture book format. Though some teachers hesitate to use illustrated versions of poems for fear of giving students interpretive clues, these books can be very useful in providing students with additional interpretations after they have experienced the poem through words alone. Student will come to realize that it is acceptable for a poem to be interpreted in a variety of ways—through art, visual images, and music.

Provide materials like the following for further exploration: *The Music of What Happens: Poems That Tell Stories* by Paul Janeczko (Orchard, 1988); *The Oxford Book* of Story Poems (Oxford, 1990); *Paul Revere's Ride* by Henry Wadsworth Longfellow illustrated by Ted Rand (Dutton, 1990); and Robert Service's *The Cremation of Sam Mcgee* (Greenwillow, 1986) and *The Shooting of Dan Mcgrew* (David R.

Godine, 1988) both illustrated by Ted Harrison. Be sure to provide versions of Asa's favorite poem, "The Highwayman" by Alfred Noyes, for students to read and hear. At least three different illustrated versions are available—by Neil Waldman (Harcourt Brace Jovanovich, 1990); Charles Mikolaycak (Oxford, 1987); and Charles Keeping (Oxford University Press, 1981). Additionally, musician/songwriter Lorena McKennit has set "The Highwayman" verses to music on her compact disc *The Book of Secrets* (Quinlan Road Music, 1997).

Life Skills (Parenting, Stepfamilies, Contemporary Issues, Divorce, Custody)

Today's students may not comprehend the obvious absence of Asa's biological father in his life. This book, set in the 1950s, reflects family relationships following divorce during that time period. Current practices involving divorce and custody situations are somewhat different. Contemporary issues include deadbeat parents (delinquent child support), joint custody arrangements, counseling, and parenting classes for stepparents. Students can explore current books, guides, and pamphlets about these issues in order to become aware of parenting responsibilities. Invite a panel of local experts (a child development specialist, judge, health and welfare official, law enforcement agent, etc.) to speak and answer questions.

Keep on Reading

Chevrolet Saturdays by Candy Dawson Boyd (Simon & Schuster, 1993). Joe has to deal with a bully, a new stepfather, and a teacher who dislikes him.

Step by Wicked Step by Anne Fine (Little, Brown, 1996). Five children tell their own stories about their wicked stepparents.

Two under Par by Kevin Henkes (Greenwillow, 1987). When Wedge's mother remarries, Wedge has to adjust to a stepfather and stepbrother.

Words of Stone by Kevin Henkes (Greenwillow, 1992). Blaze befriends a young girl who was abandoned by her mother.

A Face in Every Window by Han Nolan (Harcourt Brace, 1999). JP's fragile mother and ever-changing family taxes his emotions until he learns acceptance.

Flip-Flop Girl by Katherine Paterson (Dutton, 1994). An odd friendship develops between two lonely girls who have each lost their father.

1993
HONOR

The Dark-Thirty
Southern Tales of the Supernatural
Patricia McKissack

Plot Summary

Ten original stories based in African American history encompass the time from slavery through the Civil Rights movement. In the tradition of oral storytelling, selections include ghost stories, supernatural tales, and horror stories.

Tips

Introduce this collection of ten high-interest short stories by reading aloud the author's note (pages iii-iv, hardback edition). Each specific story is illustrated with a scratchboard drawing and preceded by a note of interest—historical information, explanations, definitions, etc.

Author Information

Born in Nashville, Patricia McKissack considers herself shaped by the Civil Rights movement of the 1960s. She and husband (and writing partner) Fredrick McKissack grew up together and married the same year they both graduated from Tennessee State University in Nashville. A love of literature and a desire to bring history alive inspire the McKissacks, and together they have written over one hundred books. Their writings reflect their African American heritage and their commitment to children and ongoing learning.

Related Author Resources

Video: *Good Conversation! A Talk with the McKissacks.* Color, 20 min. (Tim Podell Productions, 1997).

www.childrenslit.com/f_mckissack.html

www.acs.ucalgary.ca/~dkbrown/k6/mckissack.html

Book Clip

> When I was growing up in the South, we kids called the half hour just before nightfall the dark-thirty. We had exactly half an hour to get home before the monsters came out…. Then on cold winter nights, when the dark thirty came early, our family sat in the living room and talked. The talk generally led to one of Grandmama's hair-raising tales. (page iii, hardback edition)

Hold on to your hair … it's time for the dark-thirty.

Just the Facts

LC 92-3021. 122p. 1992. $15.00 (ISBN 0-679-91863-9). Knopf.

Paperback. 1996. $12 (ISBN 0-679-88335-5). Knopf.

Genres: short stories, multicultural

Themes: supernatural, spirits, ghosts, horror, African Americans, storytelling, slavery, civil rights, racism, freedom, revenge

Readability: Fifth grade

Interest Level: Fourth through ninth grade

Review Citations:

Booklist 89(8):738 Dec 15, 1992

Bulletin of the Center for Childrens Books 46(4):117 Dec 1992

Horn Book Magazine 69(2):209 Mar/Apr 1993

School Library Journal 38(12):113 Dec 1992

Publishers Weekly 239(40):96 Sept 7, 1992

Wilson Library Bulletin 67(10):102 June 1993

Curriculum Connections

Art (Scratchboard, Picture Books for Older Readers)

Illustrator Brian Pinkney uses a technique called scratchboard in which an undercoat of white clay or silver on a stiff board is covered with black and then scratched off with sharp tools. Rubbing oil pastels into the scratches created the colors added to the book jacket illustration. Students can see more of Pinkney's work in *Bill Pickett: Rodeo-Ridin' Cowboy* (Harcourt Brace, 1996); *Duke Ellington: The Piano Prince and His Orchestra* (Hyperion, 1998); and *Day of Delight: A Jewish Sabbath in Ethiopia* (Dial Books for Young Readers, 1994). Present as well work by another scratchboard artist, Michael McCurdy, with his books *Gettysburg Address* (Houghton Mifflin, 1995); *The Seasons Sewn: A Year in Patchwork* (Browndeer, 1996); *War and the Pity of War* (Clarion, 1998); and *Giants in the Land* (Houghton Mifflin, 1993).

Scratchboard art is an interesting and accessible technique for students to learn. Inexpensive commercial boards are available and artists in your community can demonstrate and teach the technique, suggest possible tools, and so on.

Related Websites

Scratchboard Tips
　www.theillustrators.com/russ/scratchtips.html

Storytelling (Folk Tales, Literature)

Even students who may not be interested in learning storytelling skills will like the idea of telling scary stories at sleepovers, slumber parties, around the campfire, and on dark and stormy nights everywhere. McKissack's collection provides excellent material for students to learn. Invite a storyteller from your community to teach the basics.

Other resources include *The Storyteller's Cornucopia* by Cathie Hilterbran Cooper (Alleyside, 1998); *Every Child a Storyteller* by Harriet R. Kinghorn and Mary Helen Pelton (Libraries Unlimited, 1991); Caroline Feller Bauer's *Read for the Fun of It: Active Programming with Books for Children* (Wilson, 1992); *Storytelling for Young Adults: Techniques and Treasury* by Gail de Vos (Libraries Unlimited, 1991); *Storytelling: Process and Practice* by Norma J. Livo and Sandra A. Rietz (Libraries Unlimited, 1986); and *Twice upon a Time* by Judy Sierra and Robert Kaminski (Wilson, 1989). Some students may wish to learn tales and stage a storytelling festival for elementary schools or public libraries. Eerie tales can be found in *Raw Head, Bloody Bones: African-American Tales of the Supernatural* by Mary E. Lyons (Aladdin, 1995) and *Ask the Bones: Scary Stories from around the World* edited by Howard Schwartz (Viking, 1999).

Related Websites

The Moonlit Road
　www.themoonlitroad.com/

History (African Americans, Research, Writing)

Most of McKissack's ten stories deal with particular events in African American history. Use these as a framework for studying African American history and learning more about each event. Examples include slavery, Rosa Parks, the Civil Rights movement, Ku Klux Klan, the Underground Railroad, black unions, etc. Helpful materials include: *The African American Experience* by Ray Spangenburg (Facts on File, 1997); *The African American Family Album* by Dorothy Hoobler (Oxford University Press, 1995); *The African-American Experience on File* by C. Carter Smith (Fact on File, 1999); *From Slave Ship to Freedom Road* by Julius Lester (Dial, 1998); and *One More River to Cross: An African American Photograph Album* by Walter Dean Myers (Browndeer, 1999).

Related Websites

The African-American Mosaic: A Library of Congress Resource Guide for the Study of Black History and Culture
　http://lcweb.loc.gov/exhibits/african/intro.html

The African American Odyssey: A Quest for Full Citizenship
　http://lcweb2.loc.gov/ammem/aaohtml/exhibit/aointro.html

Smithsonian: African American History and Culture
　www.si.edu/resource/faq/nmah/afroam.htm

Keep on Reading

Bubber Goes to Heaven by Arna Wendell Bontemps (Oxford University Press, 1998). This 1930s folktale recalls Bontemps' Southern youth.

The Phantom Hitchhiker: And Other Unsolved Mysteries by Daniel Cohen (Kingfisher, 1995). Thirteen supernatural events people claim to have experienced make up this short story collection

Restless Dead: Ghostly Tales from around the World by Daniel Cohen (Minstrel, 1996). These eleven spooky stories from other countries include tales of mummies, murder, and soldiers.

More Tales to Haunt You by Bruce Coville (Apple, 1997). This collection of ghostly tales includes a monster-hunting librarian and a ghost pig.

Raw Head, Bloody Bones: African-American Tales of the Supernatural by Mary E. Lyons (Atheneum, 1991). Ghosts, corpses, monsters, a talking skull and more haunt these fifteen scary folktales.

Scary Stories to Tell in the Dark (HarperCollins, 1981) and *More Scary Stories to Tell in the Dark* (Lippincott, 1984) both by Alvin Schwartz. These classic collections showcase hair-raising tales.

1993
HONOR

Somewhere in the Darkness
Walter Dean Myers

Plot Summary

During his sophomore year, Jimmy's life abruptly changes when his father, Crab, walks away from a prison hospital and into Jimmy's life. Hoping to clear his name and establish a relationship with his son, Crab takes Jimmy on a cross-country journey. Even though Crab has a critical illness and his re-arrest is imminent, Crab and Jimmy manage to develop a bond.

Tips

To introduce the characters and the tension, read aloud to the bottom of page 19 (paperback edition).

www.umcs.maine.edu/~orono/collaborative/somewhere.html

Book Links 2(3):41 March 1993

Author Information

Walter Dean Myers was born in 1937 in West Virginia. He came from an "absurdly" large family and was informally adopted by friends of his family who brought him to Harlem. He found his new home and family delightful and exotic. Myers had a hard time in school. He battled a speech difficulty and dropped out early on to join the army at age seventeen. After that he worked at several jobs but spent his nights writing. Proud of his Harlem heritage, Myers wants to write about this community in a realistic fashion and draws heavily on his own background and interests. An author and an editor, Myers is a member of the Harlem Writers Guild. He currently lives in Jersey City, New Jersey.

Related Author Resources

Walter Dean Myers by Diane Patrick-Wexler (Raintree/Steck Vaughn, 1995)

Walter Dean Myers: Writer for Real Teens by Denise M. Jordan (Enslow, 1999)

www.randomhouse.com/teachers/authors/myer.html

www.scils.rutgers.edu/special/kay/myers.html

www.indiana.edu/~eric_rec/ieo/bibs/myers.html

Book Links 2(5):22 May 1993

Book Clip

Having just met his father, Crab, fourteen-year-old Jimmy is traveling to an unknown destination across the country. All he knows about his absentee father is that he's been in prison for years and is now trying to clear his name. When Jimmy discovers that the police are looking for his father, he is devastated.

Just the Facts

LC 91-19295. 168p. 1992. $14.95 (ISBN 0-590-42411-4). Scholastic.

Paperback. 1993. $3.50 (ISBN 0-590-42412-2). Scholastic.

Genres: contemporary realistic fiction, multicultural

Themes: fathers and sons, self-discovery, crime, hope, prisons, death, families, deception, truancy, acceptance, music, truth, illness, daydreams

Readability: Fifth grade

Interest Level: Seventh through twelfth grade

Review Citations:

Book Report 11(2):50 Sept/Oct 1992

Booklist 99(11):1028 Feb 1, 1992

English Journal 82(8):74 Dec 1993

Horn Book Magazine 68(3):344 May 1992

Publishers Weekly 239(13):58 Mar 9, 1992

School Library Journal 38(4):146 Apr 1992

Wilson Library Bulletin 66(10):154 June 1992

Crab went back to the car and got in. Jimmy turned and walked in the opposite way. He didn't know what to do. He didn't know what to say to Crab. He didn't even know Crab …. He thought about looking for a bus station, to get back to New York, but he wasn't sure why, or why he was afraid of Crab. But he was scared, scared and tired. (pages 46–47, paperback edition)

Tired and scared—Jimmy is *Somewhere in the Darkness*.

Curriculum Connection

Sociology (Family, Fathers, Home)

The definition for family used to be fairly straightforward— a mother, father, and children. How do your students define "family"? Encourage them to come up with as many definitions as possible. Myers raises several issues concerning families. Have students identify and select topics such as the importance of active fathers, the effect of crime on families, single parent families, absent fathers, etc., for further investigation. Provide books like *The Expectant Father: Facts, Tips, and Advice for Dads-to-Be* by Armin A. Brott and Jennifer Ash (Abbeville, 1995); *101 Ways to Be a Special Dad* by Vicki Lansky (NTC/Contemporary, 1993); and *The Single Parent Resource* by Brook Noel (Champion, 1998).

Related Websites

Forum on Child and Family Statistics - Related Sites
   http://childstats.gov/related.htm

Fatherhood Initiative
   http://aspe.hhs.gov/fathers/fi-home.htm

School (Truancy, Attendance, Dropouts, Local Issues)

Jimmy has a hard time motivating himself to go to school even though he is smart. Students drop out of school for many reasons. What happens in your school? Have students interview recent and not-so-recent dropouts and compile their results. Are there some common reasons that might be addressed by changes in school policy, administration, or the courses offered? If so, encourage students to take this information to the student council, advisory boards, and/or the school administration where change may be possible.

Related Websites

High School Dropout Rates
   http://nces.ed.gov/pubs98/dropout/98250t03.html
Kids Count – Data Online
   www.aecf.org/kidscount/kc1999/defs.htm

Educational Attainment
   www.census.gov/population/www/socdemo/
   educ-attn.html

Sociology (Folk Medicine, Conjuring)

Crab consults High John, a conjurer, about his severe illness and hopes for a positive prognostication regarding his future (pages 130–140, paperback edition). Historically in the South, conjurers would commonly be consulted in cases of illness and bad luck. Materials featuring more stories and information about conjurers, voodoo, and a historical look at the South include "The Conjure Brother" in Patricia McKissack's *Dark-Thirty: Southern Tales of the Supernatural* (Knopf, 1992); *Sorrow's Kitchen: The Life and Folklore of Zora Neale Hurston* by Mary E. Lyons (Aladdin, 1993); and *Voodoo and Hoodoo: Their Tradition and Craft As Revealed by Actual Practitioners* by James Haskins (Scarborough, 1990).

Related Websites

A Cultural Outlook on the History of Black American Families in the Rural South
   www.cis.yale.edu/ynhti/curriculum/units/1990/5/90.
   05.08.x.html

Keep on Reading

Ironman: A Novel by Chris Crutcher (Dell, 1996). Beau struggles with his relationship with his father, his anger, and school.

Who Killed Mr. Chippendale? A Mystery in Poems by Mel Glenn (Dutton, 1996). Students, colleagues, and others react to the murder of a high school teacher in first-person narrative poems.

Bearstone by Will Hobbs (Atheneum, 1989). A fourteen-year-old Ute boy is given one more chance and sent to live with an old rancher in his beloved ancestors' mountains.

Where Is Home? by Jonathan London (Viking, 1995). Fourteen-year-old Aaron and his father hitchhike to San Francisco in hopes of starting a new life.

Freak the Mighty by Rodman Philbrick (Scholastic, 1993). Max lives under the shadow of his father who is serving a prison term.

Hero by Susan L. Rottman (Peachtree, 1997). An abandoned and neglected teenager is sent to perform community service at a ranch where he learns love, compassion, and respect.

1994

MEDAL

The Giver
Lois Lowry

Plot Summary

Jonas thinks his world is perfect, but he is apprehensive about the upcoming Ceremony of Twelve and wonders what his assigned vocation will be. His unusual ability to see beyond the ordinary in this futuristic society has been noticed by the Council of Elders. He is surprised and frightened by the news that he is to become the Receiver of Memory, the most highly honored job in the community. Jonas has to receive all the collective memories of their world and beyond (Elsewhere) from the Giver. The information and knowledge Jonas receives make him question his society's decision to limit choice and exclude diversity.

Tips

To bring readers into the setting, especially those unfamiliar with science fiction, read aloud through the end of chapter two. This book fosters strong opinions, and both boys and girls will be riveted by the unusual story and unresolved ending.

Related Tips

The Giver by Lois Lowry (Scholastic, 1997)

"The Inside Story: Lois Lowry's *The Giver*" by Julie Corsaro. *Book Links* 3(5):9+ May 1994

www.randomhouse.com/teachers/guides/give.html

www.sdcoe.k12.ca.us/score/giver/givertg.htm

www.eduplace.com/tview/tviews/weber1.html

www.mcdougallittell.com/lit/litcon/giver/guide.htm

Author Information

Born in Hawaii and now living in Boston and on an old farm in New Hampshire, Lowry has been a freelance writer since 1972. Many ideas for her books come from childhood memories and watching her own children. Lowry claims many of the mothers in her books are like her and when she writes she is always thinking of the child within her. She says her days are spent happily writing and reading.

The importance of passing down memories (as the Giver does to Jonas) became apparent to Lowry when her mother was dying and wanted to tell her history. When

Just the Facts

LC 92-15034. 208p. 1993. $14.95 (ISBN 0-395-64566-2). Houghton Mifflin.

Paperback. 1999. $6.99 (ISBN 0-553-7133-8). Bantam.

Audio book. Unabridged, 6 hours. 1995. $24 (ISBN 0-553-47359-X). Bantam Doubleday Dell Audio.

Genre: science fiction

Themes: dystopian society, safety, conformity, memories, truth, choices, fear, courage, interdependence, rules, ethics, freedom, euthanasia, infanticide, humanity, families, vocations

Readability: Fifth grade

Interest Level: Sixth through twelfth grade

Review Citations:

Booklist 89(16):1506 Apr 15, 1993

Bulletin of the Center for Children's Books 46(8):257 Apr 1993

English Journal 83(7):99 Nov 1994

Horn Book Magazine 69(4):458 July/Aug 1993

Publishers Weekly 240(7):240 Feb 15, 1993

School Library Journal 39(5):124 May 1993

Wilson Library Bulletin 68(2):122 Oct 1993

Lowry created the world for *The Giver* she wanted Jonas' world to seem safe and comfortable. She says "I got rid of all the things I fear and dislike: all the violence, prejudice, poverty, and injustice and I even threw in good manners as a way of life because I liked the idea of it." In 1979 Lowry photographed the painter whose picture appears on the cover of *The Giver.* While interviewing him she realized that he saw things visually that she did not. "I was grateful because he enabled me to see things differently. That aspect of someone giving me color went into the writing of the book."

Related Author Resources

Looking Back: A Book of Memories by Lois Lowry (Walter Lorraine, 1998).

www.scils.rutgers.edu/special/kay/lowry.html

www.mtnbrook.k12.al.us/wf98/llowry.htm

www.randomhouse.com/teachers/guides/lowr.html

www.ipl.org/youth/AskAuthor/Lowry.html

Newbery Acceptance Speech: *Horn Book Magazine* 70(4):414 Jul/Aug 1994

Book Clip

(Prop: A folder with a piece of paper inside containing the list on page 68.)

Every Twelve is receiving their list of instructions, telling them about their new assignments. Jonas opens his folder and reads:

> JONAS
> RECEIVER OF MEMORY
> 1. Go immediately at the end of school hours each day to the Annex entrance behind the House of the Old and present yourself to the attendant.
> 2. Go immediately to your dwelling at the conclusion of Training Hours each day.
> 3. From this moment you are exempted from rules governing rudeness. You may ask any question of any citizen and you will receive answers.
> 4. Do not discuss your training with any other member of the community, including parents and Elders.
> 5. From this moment you are prohibited from dream-telling.
> 6. Except for illness or injury unrelated to your training, do not apply for any medication.
> 7. You are not permitted to apply for release.
> 8. You may lie. (page 68, paperback edition)

You may wonder what these instructions mean. Read *The Giver* to receive the answers.

Curriculum Connections

Debate (Research, Current Events, Population Control, Euthanasia, Assisted Suicide, Death with Dignity)

To be "released" in Jonas' society is a form of population control which, in our society, would be considered euthanasia. Using current research materials, students can study the issues surrounding this controversial topic—the Oregon assisted suicide law, Dr. Kevorkian's stand about assisted suicide, and "death with dignity." Prepare pro and con arguments for these issues and stage a classic debate.

Social Studies (Society, Utopia, Dystopia, Writing)

Jonas' community is striving to be a utopia, an ideal society that exists without suffering, crime, injustice, poverty, etc. Students can read *Brave New World* by Aldous Huxley (Buccaneer, 1995) and watch the video *Pleasantville* (1998) which features a supposedly ideal world where thoughts and creativity are controlled. Students can then investigate the historic utopian communities in the United States. Discuss comparisons and contrasts, and ask students to write about their own ideal worlds.

Related Websites

The Owen/Maclure Utopian Experiment
www.usi.edu/hnh/hnh5.htm

Bishop Hill, Henry County, Illinois, USA: Utopia on the Prairie
www.outfitters.com/illinois/henry/bishop_hill.html

The Utopian Impulse
www.ipfw.indiana.edu/ipfwhist/histreso/utopian.htm

Government (Forms of Government, Rules, Freedom, Choices, Knowledge)

For Jonas and his community, there are few choices, no opportunity for change, and strict rules. This totalitarian form of government seems to work until Jonas gains knowledge and rebels. Students can study various forms of government like totalitarianism, democracy, communism, monarchies, in addition to their basic principles, and the duties and responsibilities of citizenship in each type of government. As a final project, students can write letters describing their life and civic duties to imaginary pen pals who live in non-democratic nations.

Related Websites

The Library of Congress: Country Studies
http://lcweb2.loc.gov/frd/cs/cshome.html

Governments on the WWW
www.gksoft.com/govt.

Keep on Reading

Off the Road by Nina Bawden (Clarion, 1998). Tom and his grandfather escape to the world outside the Wall when their lives are threatened in the futuristic society that eliminates old people and siblings.

Fahrenheit 451 by Ray Bradbury (Simon & Schuster, 1993). In this classic futuristic novel, firemen don't put out fires, they burn forbidden books.

The White Mountains by John Christopher (Aladdin, 1988). Will and his friends escape to the mountains to avoid the ruling Tripods and their mind control.

The Children's Story by James Clavell (Dell, 1989). A new teacher has an amazing and chilling effect on the minds of young students.

A Wrinkle in Time by Madeleine L'Engle (Farrar Straus & Giroux, 1962). Meg, her brother Charles Wallace, and friend Calvin take a perilous journey to battle an evil that threatens the universe.

The Cure by Sonia Levitin (Silver Whistle, 1999). It's the year 2407 and Gemm 16884 is too unique and emotional for this society.

1994
HONOR
Crazy Lady!
Jane Leslie Conly

Plot Summary

Along with his neighborhood buddies, Vernon sometimes taunts Maxine Flooter, a.k.a. Crazy Lady, and her retarded son, Ronald. Still grieving over his mother's death and doing poorly in school, Vernon receives tutoring from a compassionate neighbor. Her payment? Vernon is to help Maxine and Ronald. Unwittingly he becomes emotionally involved in their lives and problems.

Tips

Crazy Lady! is a fine choice to read aloud or listen to on tape. The themes provide grist for discussion and the action is sprinkled with humorous incidents. While the title alone will attract readers, teachers interested in building compassion will enjoy sharing this with students.

Author Information

Jane Leslie Conly was born in Virginia and was educated at Smith College and the Johns Hopkins Writing Seminars Program. Beginning in first grade Conly wrote stories—it was natural because her parents were writers and editors. Her first book was *Racso and the Rats of NIMH* (Harper, 1986), a sequel to her father's (John Conly O'Brien) *Mrs. Frisby and the Rats of NIMH* (Macmillan, 1971). When Conly's father learned he was going to die from heart failure, he requested that she finish his young adult novel *Z for Zachariah* (Atheneum, 1975). She has also worked as a community center and camp director and counselor. Conly says some parts of writing she likes, others she doesn't. "However, I've noticed that if I don't write a certain amount each week, I lose my overall sense of contentment." Currently Conly lives in Baltimore, Maryland, with her husband and two children.

Related Author Resources

www.carr.lib.md.us/authco/conly.htm

Book Clip

When Vernon and his friends are bored, their favorite thing to do is to tease the crazy lady who lives nearby.

> The little things we did, I guess we thought she deserved them. Like if we snitched candy, we'd always throw the wrappers in her yard. Sometimes we'd draw pictures of her on notebook paper and leave them up on the porch.

Just the Facts

LC 92-18248 196p. 1993. $15.89 (ISBN 0-06-021360-4). HarperCollins.

Paperback. 180p. 1995. $5.95 (ISBN 0-06-440571-0). HarperTrophy.

Audio book. Unabridged, 3.5 hours. 1999. $18 (ISBN 0-553-52614-6). Bantam Doubleday Dell Audio.

Genres: contemporary realistic fiction, multicultural

Themes: friendship, love, grief, neighbors, handicaps, mental retardation, alcoholism, cruelty, compassion, acceptance, family life, kindness, school work, tutoring, community, fund-raising, literacy, Special Olympics, death

Readability: Fifth grade
Interest Level: Fifth through ninth grade
Review Citations:
Booklist 89(18):1691 May 15, 1993
Bulletin of the Center for Children's Books 46(11):342 July/Aug 1993
Horn Book Magazine 69(4):465 July/Aug 1993
School Library Journal 49(4):117-18 Apr 1993

Bobby would write stuff like "You must be named Marilyn Monroe" or "I love you" on the papers. A couple of times we put fake money up against her door, hoping she'd think it was real. And another time Bobby took off his underwear and left it hanging on her doorknob. (page 16-17, hardback edition)

Who would have ever predicted that Vernon's life would become intertwined with this neighborhood character? Certainly not the *Crazy Lady!*

Curriculum Connections

Social Studies (Communities, Compassion, Fund Raising)

In order to raise money for Ronald to participate in the Special Olympics, Vernon organizes a street carnival. Students can select a cause either within their school or their community, and develop a carnival or fair to raise funds. Like Vernon they can ask for donations of baked goods, get items donated for raffles, recruit individuals to do small jobs, and so forth.

Health (Substance Abuse, Alcoholism, Families)

The Crazy Lady's behavior is primarily influenced by her abuse of alcohol, and ultimately, it is her dependence on alcohol that causes the authorities to take her son away. Students studying substance abuse and dependency can do further research on the issue of alcoholism and its effect on families. Topical books include *Drowning Our Sorrows: Psychological Effects of Alcohol Abuse* by Nancy Peacock (Chelsea House, 1999); *Hooked: Talking about Addictions* by Elaine Landau (Millbrook, 1995); *Alcohol: Opposing Viewpoints* by Scott Barbour (Greenhaven, 1997); *Everything You Need to Know about an Alcoholic Parent* by Nancy Shuker (Rosen, 1999); and *When Your Parent Drinks Too Much: A Book for Teenagers* by Eric Ryerson (Facts on File, 1985).

Related Websites

Children of Alcoholics
www.tminus10.com/children/health/factsforfamilies/childrenofalcoholics.htm

National Association for Children of Alcoholics: Questions and Answers about Addiction
www.health.org/nacoa/addictqa.htm

Sports (Special Olympics, Volunteerism)

Ronald, the Crazy Lady's son, is mentally handicapped and invited to participate in the Special Olympics. Most communities host or participate in Special Olympics programs and always need volunteers. For more information consult *Special Olympics* by Fern G. Brown (Watts, 1992).

Related Websites

Special Olympics
www.specialolympics.org/index.html

Spirit: The Magazine of Special Olympics – 30th Anniversary
www.snsgraphics.com/so_anv30/index.htm

Special Olympics Web Sites
www.cae.wisc.edu/~harrisk/Special.html

Keep on Reading

The Falcon's Wing by Dawna Lisa Buchanan (Orchard, 1992). When Bryn's father takes her to live with her cousin Winnie, who has Down's syndrome, she discovers how to cope and love.

Can You Feel the Thunder? by Lynn E. McElfresh (Atheneum, 1999). Mic lives in a neighborhood populated with weird people, including his own handicapped sister.

The King of Hearts' Heart by Sam Teague (Little, Brown, 1987). Harold helps his friend Billy make it to the Special Olympics.

The Reason for Janey by Nancy Hope Wilson (Atheneum, 1994). When Janey, a mentally disabled adult, moves in with Philly's family, things surprisingly improve.

Probably Still Nick Swansen by Virginia Euwer Wolff (Scholastic, 1997). Sixteen-year-old Nick struggles with a minimal brain dysfunction but still manages to find his way.

The Man Who Loved Clowns by June Rae Wood (Putnam, 1992). Her special needs uncle who lives with her family embarrasses Delrita.

1994
HONOR

Eleanor Roosevelt
A Life of Discovery
Russell Freedman

Plot Summary

Freedman presents Eleanor Roosevelt, a woman ahead of her time, balancing her own career with the traditional role expected of women during her lifetime. He highlights her accomplishments as a mother, First Lady, diplomat, writer, and advocate.

Tips

Many students dread the perennial biography assignment. This book, with its open format, likeable subject, and numerous photographs, will appeal to many. Also included are a photo album, bibliography, and an index. In addition, two picture book biographies can be used as introductions or supplements: *Eleanor* by Barbara Cooney (Viking, 1996) and *Amelia and Eleanor Go for a Ride: Based on a True Story* by Pam Muñoz Ryan (Scholastic, 1999).

Author Information

Russell Freedman was born in 1929 in San Francisco and graduated from the University of California - Berkeley with a major in English. After being drafted, Freedman spent two years in Korea and then began working for the Associated Press. Later he wrote television publicity for an ad agency but entertained "vague yearnings" to write books. He was inspired to write a biography of Louis Braille and his career as a writer of nonfiction for young people began.

Noted for his meticulous research, straight-forward writing style, and interesting historical characters, Russell Freedman is one of just a few Newbery winners who writes nonfiction books for children. His mission is to "capture the essence of a subject" for the readers and lead them on to explore further works on the same subject. Freedman selects his topics carefully—he has to have a personal interest in his subject matter and he wants to write about things that kids like.

Just the Facts

LC 92-25024 198p. 1993. $17.95 (ISBN 0-89919-862-7). Clarion.

Paperback. $10.95 (ISBN 0-295-84520-3). Clarion.

Audio book. Unabridged, 3.75 hours. 1997. $26 (ISBN 0-7887-1816-9)

Genres: biography, nonfiction

Themes: Eleanor Roosevelt (1884-1962), presidential wives, women's rights, politics, Great Depression, polio, war, human rights, education, family life, change, gender roles, civil rights, wealth

Readability: Seventh grade

Interest Level: Seventh through twelfth grade

Review Citations:

Booklist 89(21):1962 July 1993

Bulletin of the Center for Children's Books 47(2):44 Oct 1993

English Journal 838(7):103 Nov 1994

Horn Book Magazine 70(1):87 Jan/Feb 1994

Publishers Weekly 240(25):105

School Library Journal 39(8):196 Aug 1993

According to Freedman, Eleanor Roosevelt is a role model for both boys and girls because she took control of her own life.

Related Author Resource

www.indiana.edu/~eric_rec/ieo/bibs/freedman.html

Book Clip

To use the word "homely" to describe Eleanor Roosevelt is not really insulting. She truly wasn't a beauty. In fact, as a child she was described this way:

> "Poor little soul, she is very plain," wrote her aunt Edith. "Her mouth and teeth seem to have no future. But the ugly duckling may turn out to be a swan." (page 21, hardback and paperback edition)

Indeed, Eleanor Roosevelt turns out to be much more than a swan. She became a writer, an investigator, and an advocate for the poor and racially oppressed. Read more about her in Freedman's *Eleanor Roosevelt*.

Curriculum Connections

History (Eleanor Roosevelt, Biographies, Women, "Most Admired" lists)

Students are all too familiar with lists like "The Ten Sexiest Women (or Men)," the "Twenty-Five Most Beautiful People," etc. Eleanor Roosevelt has continually appeared on lists of the most admired women. Have students search for the "most admired" lists through reference books and the Internet. They can then learn more about the other individuals listed.

For more material and information concerning Eleanor Roosevelt refer to the following: *Eleanor Roosevelt: Freedom's Champion* (Time-Life, 1999); *Here Comes Eleanor: A New Biography of Eleanor Roosevelt for Young People* by Virginia Veeder Westervelt (Avisson, 1998); *Eleanor Roosevelt* (Great Americans: A Photobiography) edited by Nancy J. Skarmeas (Ideals, 1997); and *A Letter to Mrs. Roosevelt* by C. Coco De Young (Delacorte, 1999).

Related Websites

Women's International Center: Living Legacy Awards
  www.wic.org/misc/llaward.htm

Sara Lee Frontrunner Awards
  www.saraleefoundation.org/awards/frontrunner.htm

Dear Mrs. Roosevelt
  http://newdeal.feri.org/eleanor/index.htm

First Ladies of the United States of America
  www.whitehouse.gov/WH/glimpse/firstladies/html/firstladies.html

History (United Nations, Human Rights, Politics)

Eleanor Roosevelt was chair of the United Nations Human Rights Commission which drafted and wrote the Universal Declaration of Human Rights. The document, which has been translated into numerous languages, was referred to by Roosevelt as "a magna carta for mankind." Students can learn more about the document and discuss how relevant it is today. Provide the following for further research.

Related Websites

Universal Declaration of Human Rights
  www.unhchr.ch/udhr/index.htm

Ideas for Commemorating ... the Universal Declaration of Human Rights – Schools and Youth Organizations
  www.unhchr.ch/html/50th/ideas.htm#schools

United Nations
  www.un.org/

Speech (Public Speaking, Communication, Self-esteem)

Eleanor Roosevelt, like most people, had to learn public speaking skills when she was thrown into the limelight as the president's wife. She was somewhat shy and extremely self-conscious. Louis Howe, President Roosevelt's friend and advisor, coached Eleanor. His advice was "Have something to say, say it, and then sit down." He taught her to control her wavering voice, her nervous giggles, and to be composed. Most students could benefit from public speaking training. Invite a local debate coach and representative from Toastmasters to provide helpful hints and materials, and provide students opportunities to practice and present speeches.

Related Websites

Toastmasters International
  www.toastmasters.org/

10 Tips for Successful Public Speaking
  www.toastmasters.org/tips.htm

Keep on Reading

Herstory: Women Who Changed the World edited by Ruth Ashby and Deborah Gore Ohrn (Viking, 1995). Biographies of 120 women from prehistory to the present have been selected for *Herstory*, providing both inspiration and information.

Harriet Beecher Stowe and the Beecher Preachers by Jean Fritz (Putnam, 1998). Slavery made Harriet Beecher angry so she bucked tradition and spoke out in a time when women were supposed to be silent and obedient.

Rosa Parks: My Story by Rosa Parks with Jim Haskins (Dial, 1992). Her significant contribution to the Civil Rights movement is part of Rosa Parks' courageous story.

Ten Queens: Portraits of Women of Power by Milton Meltzer (Dutton, 1998). From Eleanor of Acquitaine to Catherine the Great, Meltzer describes ten powerful rulers who happened to be women.

Restless Spirit: The Life and Work of Dorothea Lange by Elizabeth Partridge (Viking, 1998). Talented and passionate, Dorothea Lange was dedicated to her career in photography even though family was supposed to come first.

The Flight of Red Bird: The Life of Zitkala-Sa re-created by Doreen Rappaport (Puffin, 1997). Zitkala-Sa became an activist and reclaimed her American Indian heritage after she was forced to attend boarding school.

1994

HONOR

Dragon's Gate
Laurence Yep

Plot Summary

It seemed inevitable that fourteen-year-old Otter would have a life of adventure and danger since he was born "in the hour of fire on the day of fire in the month of fire." After he accidentally kills a Manchu soldier, Otter leaves China to join his father and legendary uncle who are working on the Transcontinental Railroad in the Sierra Nevada mountains. Conditions are brutal and Otter's courage, faith, and survival instincts are put to the test.

Tips

This prequel to *Dragon Wings* (HarperCollins, 1987) contains a preface, afterword, and resource bibliography. While not recommended as a read aloud, *Dragon's Gate* serves as an excellent companion to historical studies of the Transcontinental Railroad. Read more about Otter's family in *The Serpent's Children* (HarperTrophy, 1996) and *Mountain Light* (HarperTrophy, 1997).

Related Tips

www.indiana.edu/~eric_rec/ieo/bibs/yep.html

Author Information

Newbery-winning author Laurence Yep lives in San Francisco where he grew up, and where he sets many of his books. As a kid, Yep had trouble finding characters in books he could identify with—lifestyles like those in *Homer Price* were fantasy to him. He often felt like an outsider, much like Otter in *Dragon's Gate*. While in high school Yep began writing science fiction and published his first story at the age of eighteen. Though he also writes for adult readers, Yep has special empathy with children. He says, "To write for children, one must try to see things as they do; and trying to look at the world with the fresh, inexperienced eyes of a child enables the writer to approach the world with a sense of wonder."

Related Author Resources

One of Yep's autobiographical stories is included in *When I Was Your Age: Original Stories about Growing Up* edited by Amy Ehrlich (Candlewick, 1996).

The Lost Garden by Laurence Yep (William Morrow, 1996)

www.scils.rutgers.edu/special/kay/yep.html

Just the Facts

LC 92-43649. 272p. 1993. $15.00 (ISBN 0-06-022971-3). HarperCollins.

Paperback. 1995. $5.95 (ISBN 0-06-440489-7). HarperTrophy.

Audio book. Unabridged, 7 hours. 1995. $40 (ISBN 0-7887-0132-4). Recorded Books.

Genres: historical fiction, multicultural

Themes: railroads, transcontinental railroad, Chinese laborers, survival, friendship, courage, risks, opium, avalanches, exploitation, pride, hope, strikes, immigration, adoption, freedom, accidents, death, cooperation, legends, heroes

Readability: Sixth grade
Interest Level: Sixth through ninth grade
Review Citations:
Booklist 90(9):817 Jan 1, 1994
Bulletin of the Center for Children's Books 47(4):136 Dec 1993
Horn Book Magazine 70(2):208 Mar/Apr 1994
Publishers Weekly 241(20):25 May 15, 1994
School Library Journal 40(1):135 Jan 1994

www.acs.ucalgary.ca/~dkbrown/k6/yep.html
www.indiana.edu/~eric_rec/ieo/bibs/yep.html
http://falcon.jmu.edu/~ramseyil/asialit.htm#G

Book Clip

It is winter in the Sierra Nevada mountains when fourteen-year-old Otter travels from China to work on the Transcontinental Railroad. When he arrives, he is shocked by his father and uncle's living and working conditions.

> … I gazed around the cabin. The crew looked just like corpses in narrow coffins. And overhead the storm winds howled triumphantly; and the snow … the white, white snow piled even higher above us. Uncle Foxfire straightened and looked at me without saying anything. "This mountain," I said, "kills singing. It kills laughing. It kills everything. Everyday we're here, we die a little." (page 153, hardback and paperback editions)

This mountain *will* defeat them all if they lose courage. Otter will need to find hidden strength.

Curriculum Connections

History (Chinese Americans, Culture)

The contribution of Chinese immigrants and Chinese Americans to American history is vast. Students can do further research by consulting *The Chinese American Family Album* by Dorothy Hoobler (Oxford University Press, 1998); *The Chinese Americans* by William Daley (Chelsea House, 1995); *The Chinese-American Experience* by Dana Ying-Hui Wu (Millbrook, 1993); and *Journey to Gold Mountain: The Chinese in 19th-Century America* by Rebecca Stefoff (Chelsea House, 1994); and *Tales from Gold Mountain: Stories of the Chinese in the New World* by Paul Yee (Groundwood Books, 1999).

Related Websites

Chinese American History Timeline
www.itp.berkeley.edu/~asam121/timeline.html

Chinatown Resource Guide
www.pbs.org/kqed/chinatown/resourceguide/index.html

History (Chinese Laborers, Transcontinental Railroad, Frontier, Construction)

Otter and his uncle and father were part of one of the most ambitious projects attempted in modern times.

Readers will want to learn more about all aspects of the Transcontinental Railroad. Provide them with the following: *Full Steam Ahead: The Race to Build a Transcontinental Railroad* by Rhoda Blumberg (National Geographic Society, 1996); *Tracks across America: The Story of the American Railroad, 1825–1900* by Leonard Everett Fisher (Holiday House, 1992); *The Transcontinental Railroad in American History* by R. Conrad Stein (Enslow, 1997); and *The Transcontinental Railroad: America at Its Best?* by Robert Young (Silver Burdett, 1996).

Related Websites

Union Pacific Railroad Historical Overview
www.uprr.com/uprr/ffh/history/hist-ovr.shtml

The Iron Road
www.pbs.org/wgbh/amex/iron/index.html

Steel Rails and Iron Horses
www.blm.gov/education/railroads/trans.html

Frontier Transportation
www.americanwest.com/pages/frontran.htm

Science (Weather, Avalanches, Snow)

Otter and Uncle Foxfire heroically risk their lives to save the workers' camp from a potential avalanche. Although modern weather specialists and geologists know more about avalanches now, unstable snowpack, refrozen snow, and heavy new snow continue to cause avalanches that catch victims unaware. *Landslides, Slumps, & Creep* by Peter H. Goodwin (Franklin Watts, 1997); *Avalanche Aware: Safe Travel in Avalanche Terrain* by John Moynier (Falcon, 1998); and *The Avalanche Handbook* by David McClung (Mountaineer Books, 1993) are resources for interested students. The 1999 Caldecott Award picture book, *Snowflake Bentley* by Jacqueline Briggs Martin (Houghton Mifflin, 1998) complements a study of snow crystals.

Related Websites

NOVA Online: Avalanche! Resources
www.pbs.org/wgbh/nova/avalanche/resources.html

Snow Science
www.keystone.org/school/casegoss.html

Electron Microscopy Unit Snow Page
www.lpsi.barc.usda.gov/emusnow/

Wilson A. Bentley, Photographer of Snow Crystals
http://snowflakebentley.com/

Keep on Reading

The Examination by Malcolm J. Bosse (Farrar, Straus & Giroux, 1994). Two brothers take a perilous journey across China during the Ming dynasty.

Tusk and Stone by Malcolm J. Bosse (Front Street, 1995). Set in seventh-century India, fourteen-year-old Arjun is enslaved and trained as a stonecutter.

Ajeemah and His Son by James R. Berry (HarperTrophy, 1994). Seized by slavers, Ajeemah and his son are sent to different plantations in Jamaica.

A Different Kind of Hero by Ann R. Blakeslee (Marshall Cavendish, 1997). A Chinese immigrant boy is befriended in a Colorado mining camp in the 1880s.

The Captive by Joyce Hansen (Scholastic, 1994). Kidnapped from West Africa, twelve-year-old Kafi eventually wins freedom and becomes a sailor.

No Turning Back: A Novel of South Africa by Beverley Naidoo (HarperCollins, 1997). Sipho leaves his abusive stepfather for life on the streets of Johannesburg.

1995

MEDAL

Walk Two Moons
Sharon Creech

Plot Summary

Thirteen-year-old Sal is traveling with her grandparents from Ohio to Idaho, following the same route her mother had taken earlier. On the way Sal entertains her eccentric grandparents with the story of Phoebe Winterbottom, whose mother had also left home. The telling of Phoebe's tale helps Sal come to terms with her own mother's desertion and death.

Tips

This multi-layered book, with parallel plots, may be too complex and long for a read-aloud, but many students will enjoy reading it on their own. Consider reading chapter one aloud as an introduction.

Author Information

Growing up in Ohio and later moving to England in 1979, Sharon Creech has worked as an editorial assistant and indexer at *Congressional Quarterly* in Washington, DC, and has done research for the Library of Congress archives. Currently living in Thorpe, Surrey, with her husband, Creech returns to the U.S. several times each year.

She says that *Walk Two Moons* evolved from a simple story about the Finney family to the version featuring Salamanca Tree Hiddle, and is based on much of Creech's own life. During the writing Creech was missing her own children who had returned to the U.S. to attend college and was dwelling on parent/child separations. Also interested in Native American mythology and recalling a trip her own family took from Ohio to Idaho in 1957, Creech combined all these ideas for *Walk Two Moons*. Another story about the Finney family is Creech's book *Absolutely Normal Chaos* (HarperCollins, 1995).

Related Author Resources

www.achuka.co.uk/scsg.htm

www.ala.org/alsc/creech.html

www.indiana.edu/~eric_rec/ieo/bibs/creech.html

Newbery Acceptance Speech: *Horn Book Magazine* 71(4):418 Jul/Aug 1995

Book Clip

(Prop: A white envelope with a small piece of blue paper with this message: "Don't judge a man until you've walked two moons in his moccasins.")

Just the Facts

LC 93-31277. 208p. 1994. $16 (ISBN 0-06-023334-6). HarperCollins.

Paperback. 1996. $5.95 (ISBN 0-064-40517-6). HarperTrophy.

Audio book. Unabridged. 1997. $29.98 (ISBN 0-8072-7871-8). Listening Library.

Audio book. Abridged. 1998. $16.95 (ISBN 0-694-70051-7). HarperCollins Audio.

Genre: contemporary realistic fiction

Themes: grief, abandonment, mothers, fathers, traveling, grandparents, family life, friendship, imagination, death, accidents, journal writing, codes, single parent families, school life

Readability: Fifth grade

Interest Level: Sixth through ninth grade

Review Citations:

Booklist 91(6):590 Nov 15, 1994.

Bulletin of the Center for Children's Books 48(5):162 Jan 1995

School Library Journal 40(10):142 Oct 1994

Wilson Library Bulletin 69(7):105 Mar 1995

Sal and Phoebe spend a lot of time together. Recently, a strange guy they have nicknamed "the lunatic" has been lurking about. They ...

> ... walked out onto her porch and there, lying on the top step was a white envelope. There was no name or anything on the outside. I thought it was one of those advertisements for painting your house or cleaning your carpets. Phoebe opened it. "Gosh," she said. Inside was a small piece of blue paper and on it was printed this message: [Open prop envelope and read message] (page 51, hardback edition)

Now you know where the title of this book comes from ... but who understands this unusual message?

Curriculum Connections

Art (Drawing, Comics, Caricatures)

Michael Morgan Pellowski's *The Art of Making Comic Books* (Lerner, 1995) has great appeal to kids who are either curious about comic book production or budding artists like Ben in *Walk Two Moons*. Interested students can focus their study on the visual and written development of character, plot, and setting; format, panels, and layouts; the writing process (including storyline, boxed captions, and dialogue balloons); and the art of drawing which includes practice, equipment, layout. Other helpful books include Scott McCloud's *Understanding Comics: The Invisible Art* (Kitchen Sink, 1993); Will Eisner's *Comics & Sequential Art* (Poorhouse, 1990); *Toons!: How to Draw Wild & Lively Characters for All Kinds of Cartoons* by Randy Glasbergen (North Light, 1997); *Drawing on the Funny Side of the Brain: How to Come Up with Jokes for Cartoons and Comic Strips* by Christopher Hart (Watson-Guptill, 1998); *The Art of Making Comic Books* by Michael Morgan (Lerner, 1995); and the video *The Masters of Comic Book Art* (Ken Viola Productions, 1987).

Related Websites

Gilchrist Studios Online: Drawing Lessons
  www.gilchriststudios.com/lessons/main.asp
Cynosure Arts: How to Draw Comics
  http://eet3.virtualave.net/how2draw/head1.htm

Geography (Maps, Research, Writing)

The route Sal's grandparents take from Ohio to Idaho goes through many states and includes side trips to interesting places. Using a variety of maps and atlases, students can create their own map and plot a trip, either using Sal's route and destination or selecting one of their own. Search the Web for travel information on points of interest.

Use the Vera B. Williams' picture book *Stringbean's Trip to the Shining Sea* (Greenwillow, 1988) where Stringbean and his Uncle chronicle their trip from Jeloway, Kansas, to the West Coast by sending postcards. Students can imitate the postcard format (a variation on journal writing that requires additional creativity) for a writing/art project. For additional examples provide *Postcards from Pluto: A Tour of the Solar System* by Loreen Leedy (Holiday House, 1993); *The Armadillo from Amarillo* by Lynne Cherry (Harcourt Brace, 1994); and *The Jolly Postman* by Janet Ahlberg and Allan Ahlberg (Little, Brown, 1986).

Health (Nutrition, Foods, Diet)

The Winterbottom's are zealots when it comes to eating habits, particularly concerning meat and cholesterol. Savvy students will recognize that the Winterbottoms aren't consistent and seem to consume an enormous amount of sugar and other foods considered unhealthy by some. Study reasonable, balanced diets including current recommendations. Invite a dietitian to speak to students and provide pamphlets, recipes, and health tips.

Related Websites

FDA: Center for Food Safety & Applied Nutrition
  http://vm.cfsan.fda.gov/list.html

Keep on Reading

Daddy's Climbing Tree by C.S. Adler (Clarion, 1993). Jessica is devastated when her beloved father dies.

The Not-Just-Anybody Family by Betsy Byars (Delacorte, 1986). The Blossom children live with their grandfather while their widowed mother travels the rodeo circuit.

High on the Hog by Kimberly Olson Fakih (Farrar Straus & Giroux, 1994). Trapp stays for a time on her great-grandparents' farm and discovers a family secret.

Tallahassee Higgins by Mary Downing Hahn (Harper, 1989). Talley is sent to live with her strict aunt and uncle after her mother leaves for Hollywood.

Jericho by Janet Hickman (Greenwillow, 1994). After caring for her great-grandmother, Angela begins to understand how their lives connect.

It's Nothing to a Mountain by Sid Hite (Holt, 1994). After their parents die in an accident, Lisette and Riley go to live with their grandparents in the Blue Ridge Mountains.

1995

HONOR

Catherine, Called Birdy
Karen Cushman

Plot Summary

Young teenager Catherine, nicknamed Birdy (she keeps birds as pets), is the daughter of an English knight living in the thirteenth century. She is determined not to be married off against her will and challenges her father ("the Beast") about his marriage choices and everything else. Recording her thoughts and escapades in a diary, Catherine reveals an unromantic and authentic look at the "upstairs and downstairs" of medieval life from the point of view of a spunky, intelligent young woman.

Tips

The thirteen-chapter diary is divided by months (September to September). The five-page author's note about medieval England and a bibliography are musts for teachers. Because of the diary format and subsequent lack of dialogue, *Catherine, Called Birdy* is more difficult to read than it appears. Consider introducing the book to potential readers by sharing the first chapter aloud because it sets the scene perfectly and introduces readers to the inimitable Birdy.

Related Tips

Catherine, Called Birdy by Karen Cushman (Scholastic, 1999)

www.carolhurst.com/titles/catherinecalledbirdy.html

www.eduplace.com/rdg/author/cushman/classroom.html

Author Information

Karen Cushman, an assistant director of the Museum Studies Department at John F. Kennedy University in San Francisco, has been interested in history for years. Prior to writing, Cushman read young adult historical novels and went to writers' meetings, but she was finally pushed to write by a speaker's simple suggestion: "Write from your heart." Her advice to new writers: "Go with your passion." In her fifties, Cushman has stated: "I'm a late bloomer …. It takes some time, but I always bloom."

Because Cushman is a teacher of museum studies, she has access to countless resources about medieval times. Cushman uses general histories and primary sources to collect her information. She examines firsthand accounts, letters, journals, recipes, and personal papers.

Just the Facts

LC 93-23333. 170p. 1994. $14.95 (ISBN 0-395-68186-3). Clarion.

Paperback. 212p. $5.95 (ISBN 0-06-440584-2). Harper/Trophy.

Audio book. Abridged, 3 hours. 1996. $16.99 (ISBN 0-553-47669-6). Bantam Doubleday Dell Audio.

Audio book. Unabridged, 6.5 hours. 1997. $42 (ISBN 0-7887-0687-X). Recorded Books.

Genre: historical fiction

Themes: medieval life, England, diaries, independence, gender roles, fathers and daughters, women, marriage, arranged marriages, determination, folk medicine, saints, religion, friendship, cleverness, Crusades, birds, reading, writing, love, jealousy

Readability: Seventh grade

Interest Level: Seventh through twelfth grade

Review Citations:

Booklist 90(16):1526 Apr 15, 1994

Bulletin of the Center for Children's Books 47(10):316 June 1994

Horn Book Magazine 70(4):457-58 July/Aug 1994

Publishers Weekly 241(15):66 Apr 11, 1994

School Library Journal 40(6):147 June 1994

Wilson Library Bulletin 69(4):98 Dec 1994

"Don't blow your nose in the tablecloth" was just one example of thirteenth century etiquette Cushman discovered during her research. *Catherine, Called Birdy* took her three years to finish, and the finished manuscript was accepted almost immediately. She was curious about "ordinary young people in other times" instead of the usual knights, royalty, etc.

Related Author Resources

www.eduplace.com/rdg/author/cushman/index.html

www.eduplace.com/rdg/author/cushman/classroom. html

www.eduplace.com/rdg/author/cushman/question.html

www.indiana.edu/~eric_rec/ieo/bibs/cushman.html

www.scils.rutgers.edu/special/kay/cushman.html

www.scils.rutgers.edu/special/kay/cushman5.html

www.library.ubc.ca/edlib/cushman.html

Book Clip

(Prop: Make a facsimile of a page from Birdy's diary by writing the "19th Day of September" entry in calligraphy on parchment paper.).

The year is 1290. The place is medieval England. The writer is thirteen year-old Catherine.

19th Day of September

I am delivered! My mother and I have made a bargain. I may forgo spinning as long as I write this account for Edward. My mother is not much for writing but has it in her heart to please Edward, especially now he is gone to be a monk, and I would do worse things to escape the foolish boredom of spinning. So I will write. What follows will be my book—the book of Catherine, called Little Bird or Birdy…. The writing I learned of my brother Edward, but the words are my own. Picked off twenty-nine fleas today. (page 2, hardback and paperback editions)

Curriculum Connections

History (Medieval Life, Middle Ages)

Catherine, Called Birdy portrays an unromantic, but accurate picture of everyday medieval life. This book is a natural springboard for a comprehensive classroom study or a schoolwide celebration of this fascinating time period.

The following books (including excellent picture books) will provide additional information along with details about clothing, recipes, customs, and so forth: *How Would You Survive in the Middle Ages* by Fiona MacDonald (Franklin Watts, 1997); Aliki's *A Medieval Feast* (HarperCollins, 1987); *Food & Feasts in the Middle Ages* by Imogen Dawson (New Discovery, 1994); *The Medieval Cookbook* by Maggie Black (Thames & Hudson, 1996); *Fabulous Feasts: Medieval Cookery and Ceremony* by Madeleine Pelner Cosman (Braziller, 1976); *The Oxford Illustrated History of Medieval Europe* edited by George Holmes (Oxford University Press, 1990); Sarah Howarth's *The Middle Ages* (Viking, 1993); Mitsumasa Anno's *Anno's Medieval World* (Philomel, 1979); and *Fourteenth-Century Towns* edited by John D. Clare (Harcourt Brace, 1996). Also, contact your local Society of Creative Anachronism and invite members to stage an event or share what they know about medieval customs, the art of combat, heraldry, and more.

Related Websites

The Society for Creative Anachronism
   www.sca.org/

Feudal Life: What was it Really Like to Live in the Middle Ages
   www.learner.org/exhibits/middleages/feudal.html

Internet Medieval sourcebook
   www.fordham.edu/halsall/sbook.html

Castles on the Web: Castle Tours
   www.castlesontheweb.com/search/Castle_Tours/

History (Women's Roles)

In Birdy's time the role of the woman was to be dignified, dutiful and obedient. Girls were married off not for love, but as a matter of economics. Birdy describes "lady-lessons" in the "8th Day of May" entry. Using this information, students can research women in this period and compare their lives to women's roles in other societies and cultures, both in the past and present. An appropriate time to focus this study would be in March during Women's History Month.

Related Websites

Dominion & Domination of the Gentle Sex: The Lives of Medieval Women
   http://library.advanced.org/12834/index.html

Dominion & Domination of the Gentle Sex: The Distaff Side
   http://library.advanced.org/12834/text/distaffside. html

Medieval Domestic Life
   www.millersv.edu/~english/homepage/duncan/
   medfem/domestic.html

Woman's History
   www.feminist.org/other/wh_menu.html

Writing (Diaries, Journals, Autobiographies)

Readers get a clear idea of Birdy's everyday life thorough the personal nature of her diary entries. Provide students with real and fictitious diaries and journals such as *A Gathering of Days: A New England Girl's Journal, 1830–32* by Joan W. Blos (Atheneum, 1980); *For Your Eyes Only!* by Joanne Rocklin (Scholastic, 1997); *The Music of Dolphins* by Karen Hesse (Scholastic, 1996); *Children in the Holocaust and World War II: Their Secret Diaries* by Laurel Holliday (Pocket Books, 1995); *The Diary of a Young Girl: The Definitive Edition* by Anne Frank and edited by Otto H. Frank (Doubleday, 1995); *Zlata's Diary: A Child's Life in Sarajevo* by Zlata Filipovic (Penguin, 1995); and *Running Girl: The Diary of Ebonee Rose* by Sharon Bell Mathis (Harcourt Brace, 1997).

Encourage students to keep daily or weekly (real-life or fictitious) journals themselves. Provide the following how-to-resources to help students begin a journal or diary: *All about Me: A Keepsake Journal for Kids* by Linda Kranz (Rising Moon, 1996); *A Book of Your Own: Keeping a Diary or Journal* by Carla Stevens (Clarion, 1993); and *The Book of Myself: A Do-It-Yourself Autobiography in 201 Questions* by Carl Marshall (Hyperion, 1997).

Related Websites

The Diary Project
   www.diaryproject.com/about.shtml

The Vermont Historical Society: Using Historical Journals in the Classroom
   www.state.vt.us/vhs/educate/diaries.htm

The Story of the Diary
   http://annefrank.com/anne/diary/diary.html

A Teacher's Guide to the Holocaust: Diaries and Memoirs
   http://fcit.coedu.usf.edu/holocaust/activity/plans1/
   diaries.htm

Keep on Reading

Anna of Byzantium by Tracy Barrett (Delacorte, 1999). Although Anna is heir to the emperor, events intervene and her future becomes uncertain.

The Outlaws of Sherwood by Robin McKinley (Ace Books, 1989). The adventures of Robin Hood and his merry men are retold in novel fashion.

The Juggler by John Morressy (Harper Trophy, 1998). A medieval boy named Beran makes a pact with the devil to become the greatest juggler ever.

Crown Duel by Sherwood Smith (Harcourt Brace, 1997). The Countess Meliara works with her brother to free her country from an oppressive enemy in this medieval fantasy.

The Ramsay Scallop by Frances Temple (Orchard, 1994). Eleanor is reluctant to marry Lord Thomas after he returns from his crusade to the Holy Land.

Child of the May by Theresa Tomlinson (Orchard, 1998). Magda, apprentice to a midwife, wants to leave the woods but ends up helping Robin Hood in a daring rescue.

1995
HONOR
The Ear, the Eye and the Arm
Nancy Farmer

Plot Summary

General Matsika, Chief of Security for Zimbabwe in the year 2194, has created a fortified home for the safety of his family. His three children resent these restrictions and long to have everyday experiences. With the help of the family Mellower, the family's Praise Singer, thirteen year-old Tendai, eleven-year-old Rita, and their four-year-old brother Kuda sneak out for a forbidden adventure. Plans to return that day abruptly change when they are kidnapped. Disaster follows disaster as they courageously escape from a variety of villains and evil spirits of the past. Meanwhile, the three specially talented mutant detectives (the Ear, the Eye and the Arm), hired by the General's wife nearly rescue the children several times while having their own adventures in the process. An evil gang, intent on sacrificing the children, is defeated when Tendai calls on his own personal strength and spiritual connections. African folklore meets futuristic technology.

Tips

An epilogue, a glossary and a nine-section appendix complement the 40 chapters, which greatly enhance the understanding and enjoyment of *The Ear, the Eye and the Arm*. Introduce the book using the Book Clip on the next page.

Related Tips

Aaron Shepard's Reader's Theater: Resthaven by Nancy Farmer
   www.aaronshep.com/rt/index.html

Author Information

Born in Arizona, Nancy Farmer grew up surrounded by storytelling and is now a professional storyteller herself. She attended the University of California and worked as a lab technician in Berkeley. Her varied careers include joining the Peace Corps and going to India, and working as a chemist and entomologist in Zimbabwe where she met her husband. Farmer lived in Africa for seventeen years and says her experiences there had a major effect on her writing. Her rules for becoming a successful writer are: "(1) Read as much as possible, (2) Write as much as possible for several years, and (3) Submit manuscripts to a wide variety of editors." Farmer now lives with her family in California.

Just the Facts

LC 93-11814. 320p. 1994. $18.95 (ISBN 0-531-06829-3) library binding $17.99 (ISBN 0-531-08679-8). Orchard Books.

Paperback. 1995. $4.99 (ISBN 0-14-037641-0). Puffin Books.

Audio book. Unabridged, 10 hours. 1995. $55 (ISBN 0-788-70431-1). Recorded Books.

Genres: science fiction, adventure, multicultural

Themes: kidnapping, detectives, resourcefulness, Zimbabwe, African culture, good versus evil, heroes, toxic waste, recycling, technology, criminals, security, superhuman powers, mutations, futuristic world, robots, gangs, storytelling, slaves, witchcraft, military training

Readability: Sixth grade

Interest Level: Seventh through twelfth grade

Review Citations:

Booklist 90(15):1436 Apr 1, 1994

Bulletin of the Center for Children's Books 47(7):221 Mar 1994

Horn Book Magazine 70(5):597-98 Sept/Oct 1994

Publishers Weekly 241(15):66 APR 11, 1994

School Library Journal 40(6):147 June 1994

Book Clip

Mother has hired three strange detectives, the Ear, the Eye and the Arm, to find her missing children. This is her first encounter with them.

> The three men stood in front of Mother and let her take a long look. Ear, who was white, unfolded his ears. They opened out like huge flowers, pink and almost transparent. Eye, who was brown, blinked his huge eyes, which were all pupil inside and no white. Arm, who could just as well have been called Leg, stretched out his long black limbs. He reminded Mother of a wall spider.
>
> "How—how did you happen?" she asked.
>
> Arm replied, "We all come from the village of Hwange, near the nuclear power plant."
>
> "Oh yes," said Mother. "That's where the plutonium got into the drinking water."
>
> "Our mothers drank it."
>
> "Our parents were delighted when they found out what we could do," said Eye …"I could see a flea clinging to a hawk's feathers. My mother never lost anything."
>
> "I could hear an ant creeping up on a sugar bowl," boasted Ear ….
>
> "I got hunches," Arm said. "I used to know when the baboons were planning to raid the fields. So you see, we were ideally suited to become detectives." (page 50, hardback and paperback editions)

It will take real detectives to locate the kidnapped children. Are *The Ear, the Eye and the Arm* up to the challenge?

Curriculum Connections

History (Current Events)

A futuristic picture of life in Zimbabwe is portrayed in *The Ear, the Eye and the Arm*. For now, however, students will get a current understanding of the country and its cultures by reading the book's appendices and studying the country through newspapers, periodicals, televised reports, and Internet sites.

Related Websites

University of Pennsylvania African Studies Center: Zimbabwe
   www.sas.upenn.edu/African_Studies/Country_ Specific/Zimbabwe.html

Africa Online: Zimbabwe
   www.africaonline.co.zw/

Zimbabwe
   www.zimweb.com/Dzimbabwe.html

Science (Environment, Toxic Waste, Mutations, Superfund Cleanup Sites)

The Vlei people live on a wasteland where toxic chemicals had been dumped. The contamination ruined a large area in the middle of the city and the only people who remained were rejected humans who were unwanted elsewhere. Farmer frames a cautionary tale about the dangers of toxic waste accumulation and nuclear accidents that could result in mutations such as those exhibited by the Ear, the Eye and the Arm.

Is there a superfund or toxic waste accumulation site in your area or nearby? Investigate a super fund or toxic waste cleanup situation. What are the potential dangers? What can citizens do to prevent future problems? Students who are interested in pursuing a study of these issues can refer to *Chattanooga Sludge: Cleaning Toxic Sludge from Chattanooga Creek* by Molly Bang (Gulliver Books, 1996); *Toxic Materials* by Richard Amdur (Chelsea House, 1993); and *The Complete Guide to Hazardous Waste Regulations: RCRA, TSCA, HMTA, OSHA, and Superfund* by Travis P. Wagner (John Wiley, 1999).

Related Websites

Environmental Protection Agency: Superfund
   www.epa.gov/superfund/

Environmental Protection Agency: Superfund Regions
   www.epa.gov/superfund/regions/index.htm

Science (Robotics)

In the futuristic world of *The Ear, the Eye and the Arm*, robots serve the General and his family in the capacity of guard dogs, butlers, gardeners, and maids. Students can research the extent to which robots are currently used. If possible, invite someone in your area who has developed a robot and can demonstrate its use at your school. Encourage students to build their own robots and provide books like the following: *Mobile Robots: Inspiration to Implementation* by Joseph L. Jones, Anita M. Flynn, and Bruce A. Seiger (A K Peters, 1998) and *The Robot Builder's Bonanza: 99 Inexpensive Robotics Projects* by Gordon McComb (TAB, 1987).

For further research into the increasing use of robots, students can refer to *Artificial Intelligence: Robotics and Machine Evolution* by David Jefferis and Davies

Jefferis (Crabtree, 1999); *Robotics: The Marriage of Computers and Machines* by Ellen Thro (Facts on File , 1993); and the unusual *Action Robots: A Pop-Up Book Showing How They Work* by Tim Reeve (Gavin MacLeod, 1995).

Related Websites

RobotBooks.com
   www.robotbooks.com/

Lego: Mindstorms – Robot News & Links, etc.
   www.legomindstorms.com/

Computer Motion
   www.computermotion.com/

Keep on Reading

AK by Peter Dickinson (Laurel-Leaf, 1994). In the mythical African nation of Nagala, Paul is raised to battle the enemy.

Eva by Peter Dickinson (Laurel-Leaf, 1990). When Eva awakens after a terrible accident, she discovers she has been given the body of a chimpanzee.

Running Out of Time by Margaret Peterson Haddix (Simon & Schuster, 1995). Jessie thinks she lives in the 1840s in a small secluded village but she's the only one who can escape to the present and save her family.

Invitation to the Game by Monica Hughes (Aladdin, 1993). In the year 2154 this group of teenagers receive an invitation to the Game—a computer-generated survival test.

Galax-Arena by Gillian Rubinstein (Simon & Schuster, 1995). Kidnapped from an Australian train station in the year 2025, three siblings become prisoners in Galax-Arena.

Gypsyworld by Julian Thompson (Henry Holt, 1992). A parallel world to Earth, Gypsyworld is the place where five teenagers are taken, and where they learn about true ecological balance.

1996 MEDAL

The Midwife's Apprentice
Karen Cushman

Plot Summary

A sharp-tongued midwife takes in a homeless waif and the metamorphosis of this young girl from Brat to Beetle to Alyce commences. Alyce learns the folk-healing skills of a medieval midwife and ultimately develops her own self-identity and talents.

Tips

This short, pithy 122-page novel, with small pages and good-sized print, is a great choice for independent reading. Introduce with the Book Clip here or read aloud chapter one to launch readers.

Related Tips

www.eduplace.com/rdg/author/cushman/classroom. html

www.eduplace.com/tview/tviews/smith49.html

www.westga.edu/~kidreach/midwife.html

www.soemadison.wisc.edu/ccbc/midwife.htm

www.eduplace.com/tview/tviews/smith49.html

Author Information

Karen Cushman, an assistant director of the Museum Studies Department at John F. Kennedy University in San Francisco, has been interested in history for years. Prior to writing, Cushman read young adult historical novels and went to writers' meetings, but she was finally pushed to write by a speaker's simple suggestion: "Write from your heart." Her advice to new writers: "Go with your passion." In her fifties, Cushman has stated: "I'm a late bloomer .... It takes some time, but I always bloom."

Because Cushman is a teacher of museum studies, she has access to countless resources about medieval times. Cushman uses general histories and primary sources to collect her information. She examines firsthand accounts, letters, journals, recipes, and personal papers.

Related Author Resources

www.eduplace.com/rdg/author/cushman/index.html

www.eduplace.com/rdg/author/cushman/classroom. html

www.eduplace.com/rdg/author/cushman/question.html

www.indiana.edu/~eric_rec/ieo/bibs/cushman.html

Just the Facts

LC 94-13792. 122p. 1995. $10.95 (ISBN 0-395-69229-6). Clarion.

Paperback. 1996. $5.95 (ISBN 0-06-440630-X). Harper/Trophy.

Audio book. Lightly abridged, 2 hours. 1996. $16.99 (ISBN 0-553-47798-6). Bantam Doubleday Dell Audio.

Audio book. Unabridged, 2.75 hours. 1996. $18 (ISBN 0-788-70577-6). Recorded Books.

Genre: historical fiction

Themes: medieval life, England, gender roles, midwifery, folk medicine, birth and birthing, self-esteem, apprenticeships, homelessness, superstitions, herbs, orphans, reading, literacy, hunger, witches, greed, kindness, belonging, names

Readability: Seventh grade

Interest Level: Seventh through twelfth grade

Review Citations:

Booklist 91(14):1328 Mar 15, 1995

Bulletin of the Center for Children's Books 48(9):303 May 1995

English Journal 85(7):131 Nov 1996

Horn Book Magazine 71(4):465-66 July/Aug 1995

Publishers Weekly 242(9):104 Feb 27, 1995

School Library Journal 41(5):118 May 1995

www.scils.rutgers.edu/special/kay/cushman.html

www.scils.rutgers.edu/special/kay/cushman5.html

www.library.ubc.ca/edlib/cushman.html

Newbery Acceptance speech: *Horn Book Magazine* 72(4):413 July/Aug 1996

www.eduplace.com/rdg/author/cushman/newbery.html

Book Clip

Magister Reese takes kindly to young Alyce and surreptitiously teaches her how to read. He knows she is quick and smart and deserves a better life than that of a servant. He wonders aloud what she wants from life.

> Alyce stopped still. She thought just to sweep away, but the shock of his addressing her directly was lost in that intriguing question. What did she want? … She chewed on a lock of her hair to help her think. What did people want? Blackberry pie? New shoes? A snug cottage and a bit of land? She thought all that wet afternoon and finally, as she served Magister Reese his cold-beef-and-bread supper, she cleared her throat a time or two and then softly answered: "I know what I want. A full belly, a contented heart, and a place in this world."(pages 80-81 hardback edition)

Maybe finding a place in this world is not impossible. Read *The Midwife's Apprentice* to see if Alyce gets what she wants.

Curriculum Connections

Careers (Apprenticeships, Colleges, Jobs, Interviews, Applications, Work)

Alyce ultimately realizes that she is smart enough to learn a trade, and she understands that becoming successful in a job is essential to finding satisfaction and a place in the world. Like Alyce, students need to look ahead toward some sort of higher education or future training. Some programs like "Service Learning" and "School to Work" help students begin preparation for careers while they are still in school. For college-bound students there are many guides available to assist in selecting and applying for colleges. Helpful books include both the *East* (1999) and *West* (2000) edition of *Peterson's Vocational and Technical Schools and Programs* edited by Jon Latimer (Petersons Guides, 1997); *Guide to Alternative Education and Training* by Vivian DuBrovin (Watts, 1988); and *Choices for the High School Graduate: A*

Survival Guide for the Information Age by Bryna J. Fireside (Ferguson, 1999).

Related Websites:

FutureQuest
www.pvpusd.k12.ca.us/teachweb/twidwelll/FutureQuest.html

The Hot Seat: Mock Job Interview
www1.kaplan.com/view/article/0,1898,3134,00.html

US News Online: 2000 College Rankings
www.usnews.com/usnews/edu/college/corank.htm

SLJ Online- Surf For: College Craze
www.schoollibraryjournal.com/articles/surffor/19980801_5848.asp

CareerPath.com
www.careerpath.com

The Employment Guide's Career Web
www.cweb.com

Cool Works
www.coolworks.com/showme/

Careers (Midwives)

Throughout history, midwives have been essential in communities. Interested students may wish to learn more about midwifery as a career. In many states a certified nurse midwife is considered a primary care provider, offering another option for normal pregnancy, childbirth, postpartum and gynecological needs for women, even though the majority of midwife-attended births actually occur in hospitals.

Related Websites

American College of Nurse-Midwives
www.midwife.org/

The ParentsPlace: Pregnancy and birth Reading Room
www.parentsplace.com/readroom/pregnant.html#midwife

Midwifery Today with the International Midwife
www.midwiferytoday.com/

Health (Folk Medicine, Herbs)

One of Alyce's jobs is to collect various herbs for the midwife's patients. Herb lore and folk medicine have become increasingly of interest to many individuals. Make the following reference books available for further information: *Rodale's Illustrated Encyclopedia of Herbs* by Claire Kowalchik and William H. Hylton (Rodale, 1998); *Deni Bown's Encyclopedia of Herbs and Their Uses* (Dorling Kindersley, 1995); *The*

History and Folklore of North American Wildflowers by Timothy Coffey (Houghton Mifflin, 1994); *Folk Remedies That Work* by Joan Wilen and Lydia Wilen (HarperPerennial Library, 1996); *Pharmacy in the Forest: How Medicines Are Found in the Natural World* by Fred Powledge (Atheneum, 1998); and *Poisons in Our Path: Plants That Harm and Heal* by Anne Ophelia Dowden (HarperCollins, 1994).

Related Websites

Curriculum Materials: Chemistry of Folk Remedies
  www.ael.org/nsf/voices/curric/folk.htm

America Botanical Council
  www.herbalgram.org/

Keep on Reading

The Borning Room by Paul Fleischman (HarperTrophy, 1993). Births and deaths and all in between takes place in the borning room on this Ohio farm.

Wise Child by Monica Furlong (Knopf, 1987). No one wants the abandoned Wise Child except the gentle Juniper, a healer who lives on the outskirts of town.

Juniper by Monica Furlong (Random House, 1992). This prequel to Wise Child tells the story of Juniper who becomes a wise and wonderful healer.

Dove and Sword: A Novel of Joan of Arc by Nancy Garden (Farrar Straus & Giroux, 1995). Young Gabrielle was learning to be a midwife when she disguises herself as a boy to follow Jeannette's army.

Raging Quiet by Sherryl Jordan (Simon & Schuster, 1999). After her drunken husband dies, sixteen-year-old Marnie is hated by the suspicious villagers.

The Forestwife by Theresa Tomlinson (Orchard, 1995). Fifteen-year-old Marian cannot marry the young outlaw Robert because she must take the place of Agnes, the midwife.

1996

HONOR

What Jamie Saw
Carolyn Coman

Plot Summary

Jamie's mother miraculously catches the baby thrown by her boyfriend. The trauma of that event plus the subsequent poverty, fear, and isolation nearly incapacitate nine-year-old Jamie and his mother. Fortunately a caring teacher intervenes and Jamie's mother begins to take control.

Tips

Many readers won't self-select this book because the main character is so young. However, the book is written for a young adult audience so teachers and librarians need to make that clear when they "sell" the book. Other options include reading aloud the first page to hook readers, or sharing this short and sophisticated book in its entirety.

Related Tips

www.write4kids.com/feature6.html

Author Information

Born in Chicago, Carolyn Coman graduated with the first class of Hampshire College in Amherst, Massachusetts. For some years she worked as an editor and hand bookbinder. Now she lives in Newburyport, Massachusetts, with her two children and writes fulltime. Several little boys Coman observed when she was volunteering in her daughter's classroom inspired the character of Jamie. He was named after a courageous high school girl Coman taught who succeeded against great odds.

Book Clip

In the night, something awakens nine-year-old Jamie.

> It wasn't the crying that woke him up. It was some other sound—what was it?—something else that made him spring up in bed, lean back on his elbows, and open his eyes wide, just in time to see Van reach into the crib and grab Nin and throw her, fire her across the room, like a missile, like a bullet, like a shooting star, like a football. No: like nothing Jamie'd ever seen before. (page 9, paperback edition)

That's what Jamie saw.

Just the Facts

LC 95-23545. 126p 1995.$13.95 (ISBN 1-886-91002-2). Front Street.

Paperback. $4.99 (ISBN 0-14-038335-2). Puffin Books.

Genre: contemporary realistic fiction

Themes: child abuse, single parent families, poverty, friendship, siblings, fear, anger, self-control, domestic violence, choices, hiding, school life, hope, magic tricks, fantasy, teachers, smoking

Readability: Fifth grade

Interest Level: Fifth through eighth grade

Review Citations:

Booklist 92(8):703 Dec 15, 1995

Bulletin of the Center for Children's Books 49(4):123 Dec 1995

Horn Book Magazine 72(2):104 Mar/Apr 1996

Publishers Weekly 242(35):114 Aug 28, 1995

School Library Journal 41(12):128 Dec 1995

Curriculum Connections

Current Issues (Child Abuse, Violence, Statistics, Counseling)

Unfortunately, Jamie's young sister is one of many child abuse victims. Students can find national, state, and local statistics. What programs are available in your area for child abuse victims? Invite an informed speaker to talk to your class about this troubling issue, and encourage students to learn more about your local statistics and programs, treatment of child abuse, neglect prevention, and general child welfare.

Related Websites

Family Violence Prevention Fund
    www.fvpf.org

Kids count - Data Online
    www.aecf.org/kidscount/kc1999/defs.htm

Hobbies (Magic, Magic Tricks)

When his world is topsy-turvy, Jamie finds solace in practicing and performing magic tricks. Even students with calm lives might enjoy learning and performing magic. Helpful materials include *101 Classic Magic Tricks* by Guy Frederick (Sterling, 1995); *Easy-to-Do Magic Tricks for Children* by Karl Fulves (Dover, 1993); and *The Klutz of Magic* by John Cassidy et al. (Klutz, 1989).

Related Websites

The Case.com for Kids — Magic
    www.thecase.com/kids/magic/

Just for Fun: Magic Tricks
    www.wannalearn.com/Just_for_Fun/Magic_Tricks/

Life Skills (Parenting)

Despite her circumstances, Jamie's mother is trying to be the best parent she can be even though it seems likely she is operating by instinct only. Most individuals receive no parenting training—the most important job they'll ever have. In preparation for potential parenthood, students can learn why babies like Nin cry, find out about the importance of play, and learn age-appropriate activi-ties. Provide books like *Touchpoints: Your Child's Emotional and Behavioral Development* by T. Berry Brazelton, M.D. (Perseus, 1994); *The New Parent* by Miriam Stoppard (DK, 1998); *Making It Better: Activities for Children Living in a Stressful World* by Barbara Oehlberg (Redleaf, 1996).

Related Websites

National Parent Information Network
    http://npin.org/links.html

Kid Source Online — Parenting
    www.kidsource.com/kidsource/pages/parenting.html

Multnomah County Library Electronic Resources: Parenting
    www.multnomah.lib.or.us/lib/ref/parent.html

Keep on Reading

3 NBs of Julian Drew by James M. Deem (Houghton Mifflin, 1994). His neglectful father and cruel stepmother victimize fifteen-year-old Julian Drew.

Dancing on the Edge by Han Nolan (Harcourt Brace, 1997). Miracle, saved at birth, struggles to find out the family truths among the lies.

Don't You Dare Read This, Mrs. Dumphrey by Margaret Peterson Haddix (Simon & Schuster, 1996). Tish writes in her journal about her abusive father, depressed mother, and their abandonment of Tish and her younger brother.

Hero by Susan L. Rottman (Peachtree, 1997). After having problems at school, Sean is taken from his abusive mother and sent to a ranch to perform community service.

Double or Nothing by Marc Talbert (Dial, 1990). Even after he died Sam always remembered his Uncle Frank who was a professional magician and Sam's friend.

Make Lemonade by Virginia Euwer Wolff (Henry Holt, 1994). Teen parent Jolly needs help to take care of her two young children.

1996
HONOR

The Watsons Go to Birmingham — 1963

Christopher Paul Curtis

Plot Summary

The Watsons are a close-knit family who enjoy life, music, and emerging technology in the 60s. Sibling rivalry abounds among ten-year-old Kenny, his older brother and younger sister. Like many African American families, the Watsons have strong ties to the South and that's where they head for their summer vacation. The tension of the times requires careful travel planning in order to avoid racially charged incidents. The parents decide not to leave older brother Byron in Birmingham with his strict grandmother after racial violence results in the bombing of a neighborhood church.

Tips

This is an excellent read-aloud during a study of the Constitution and Civil Rights. The book includes fifteen chapters, an epilogue, and an unusual dedication.

Related Tips

www.randomhouse.com/teachers/guides/wats.html

www.umcs.maine.edu/~orono/collaborative/watsons.html

www.westga.edu/~kidreach/watsons.html

Author Information

Although he felt a burning desire to write, Curtis took a job hanging doors on cars after graduating from high school and kept this job for thirteen years. His wife pushed him back to writing saying "better hurry up and start doing something constructive … or look for a new place to live."

Like his protagonist Kenny, Christopher Paul Curtis grew up in Flint, Michigan. Curtis won the Avery Hopwood Prize for major essays and the Jules Hopwood Prize for an early version of *The Watsons Go to Birmingham—1963*, which eventually became Curtis' first novel. His novel Bud, Not Buddy (Delacorte, 1999) won the 2000 Newbery Award.

Related Author Resources

www.randomhouse.com/teachersbdd/curt.html

Book Clip

The Watson's neighbor, Mrs. Davidson, really has a soft

Just the Facts

LC 95-7091 210p. 1995. $14.95 (ISBN 0-385-32175-9). Delacorte.

Paperback. 1997. $5.50 (ISBN 0-440-41412-1). Bantam.

Audio book. Abridged, 5 hours. 1996. $18.99 (ISBN 0-553-47786-2). Bantam Doubleday Dell Audio.

Genres: historical fiction, multicultural

Themes: African Americans, family life, prejudice, brothers and sisters, friendship, bullies, racism, summer vacations, grandparents, Civil Rights, bombings, reading

Readability: Upper fifth grade

Interest Level: Fifth through eighth grade

Review Citations:

Booklist 91(22):1946 Aug 1995

Bulletin of the Center for Children's Books 49(5):157 Jan 1996

Horn Book Magazine 72(2):195 Mar/Apr 1996

Publishers Weekly 242(42):62 Oct 16, 1995

School Library Journal 41(10):152 Oct 1995

spot for little Joey and decides to give her a gift ... a little chubby angel. Momma wonders why Joey is less than thrilled.

"What was wrong?"

"That angel, Mommy."

"Oh?"

"Mrs. Davidson said it reminded her of me, but it didn't look like me at all."...Momma went and got the angel and sat next to Joey.

"Sweetheart, I can see how it reminds her of you. Look at that dimple."

"But Mommy, it's white." (page 128, hardback edition)

Living in the United States in 1963 was difficult for many African Americans. Wait until you see what else happens when *The Watsons Go to Birmingham*.

Curriculum Connections

Social Studies (Fashion, Culture, African Americans, Hair)

"Byron had gotten a conk! A process! A do! A butter! A ton of trouble!" (page 87, hardback edition) Momma is furious about Byron's new haircut. Hairstyles change all the time and the cultural, behavioral, and societal aspects of these changes can be fascinating. Having the "right" hair from "conk" to "Afro" has always been important. Read the picture books, *Nappy Hair* by Carolivia Herron (Knopf, 1997) and *Happy to Be Nappy* by bell hooks (Hyperion, 1999) to your students. Collect a group of books that deal specifically with African American hair like *Hair Raising: Beauty, Culture, and African American Women* by Noliwe M. Rooks (Rutgers University Press, 1996) and *Healthy Hair Care Tips for Today's Black Woman* by Cheryl Talley Moss (Talley, 1999).

History (Civil Rights, Research, Violence, Bombings, Arson)

Curtis writes dramatically about the church bombing in Alabama. Many students may not know that the September 15, 1963, bombing of the Sixteenth Baptist Church in Birmingham, Alabama, actually happened in the midst of the Civil Rights struggles in the 1960s. Unfortunately 30 years later in 1996 there were a series of arson fires in African American churches. These ongoing acts remind us of continuing racial conflicts. Prompt students to research and report on hate crimes, violence toward minorities, and other Civil Rights issues—both historical and contemporary.

Related Websites

Birmingham Bombing
www.dc.peachnet.edu/~yliu/papr/birmingham.htm

History of Church Fires
www.washingtonpost.com/wp-srv/national/longterm/churches/photo3.htm

Journey to Peace: Links
www.useekufind.com/peace/links.htm

Historian says church arsons are nothing new for blacks in America
www.brown.edu/Administration/News_Bureau/1995-96/95 171i.html

Language Arts (Langston Hughes, Author Studies, Biographies, Poetry, Reading Aloud, Picture Books for Older Readers)

Kenny reads aloud wonderfully and is asked to read aloud a selection from Langston Hughes in class. Though known mainly as a poet, Hughes also wrote essays, plays, short stories and novels. Present students with a variety of illustrated books featuring the work of Hughes including *The Dream Keeper and Other Poems* (Knopf, 1994); *Black Misery* (Oxford University Press, 1994); *The Sweet and Sour Animal Book* (Oxford University Press, 1997); and *The Block: Poems* (Viking, 1995). In addition, provide students with S.L. Berry's *Langston Hughes* (Creative Education, 1994); Floyd Cooper's *Coming Home: From the Life of Langston Hughes* (Philomel, 1994); and *Free to Dream: The Making of a Poet, Langston Hughes* by Audrey Osofsky (Lothrop, Lee & Shepard, 1996).

Related Websites

Langston Hughes (1902-1967)
www.hmco.com/college/english/heath/syllabuild/iguide/hughes.html

Smithsonian Institution: Langston Hughes and the Harlem Renaissance
www.si.edu/tsa/disctheater/sweet/tss03.htm

Langston Hughes (1902-1967): Teacher Resource File
http://falcon.jmu.edu/~ramseyil/hughes.htm

Keep on Reading

Starplace by Vicki Grove (Putnam, 1999). Frannie Driscoll finds out about segregation and past atrocities of the Ku Klux Klan in her Oklahoma town.

Mayfield Crossing by Vaunda Micheaux Nelson (Putnam, 1993). When their school is closed, the

Mayfield Crossing kids have to attend an all-white school and experience racism for the first time.

Hold Fast to Dreams by Andrea Davis Pinkney (William Morrow, 1995). The only black student in her middle school, Dee tries to adjust.

Speed of Light by Sybil Rosen (Simon & Schuster, 1999). Segregation becomes an issue in a small Virginia town in 1956.

Dangerous Skies by Suzanne Fisher Staples (Farrar, Straus & Giroux, 1996). Even though he is white, Buck has been best friends with Tunes, an African American girl—until they uncover a crime and race becomes an issue.

Suitcase by Mildred Pitts Walter (Lothrop, Lee & Shepard, 1999). An overly tall African American boy gains self-esteem and his father's love as he develops his artistic and athletic talents.

1996 HONOR

Yolonda's Genius

Carol Fenner

Plot Summary

Violence and crime cause ten-year-old Yolonda's mother to relocate from Chicago to a smaller city in Michigan. While Yolonda's adjustment is somewhat difficult with her peers, she continues to be successful in school and becomes aware of her younger brother's musical genius. Seizing an opportunity, Yolonda schemes to have his talent discovered at a blues concert.

Tips

The eighteen chapters are large print and include an author's note about the Chicago Music Festivals. Hook potential readers by reading aloud the first paragraph, and by providing recordings of Chicago blues music.

Author Information

Carol Fenner's first poem was about dandelions and it came to her when she was just five years old. Her mother wrote it down for her and continued to pen Fenner's creations until she could write them herself. Fenner's love of words and stories is attributed to her mother (who read poems aloud at bedtime), and her Aunt Phyllis—a librarian who brought Fenner and her siblings a steady supply of wonderful books. Fenner credits her husband, an inveterate lover of live blues and jazz, with helping her discover the character and essence of Yolonda.

Book Clip

By reading the dictionary at the public library, Yolonda learns that a true "genius" is one who re-arranges old material. Finally she understands her six-year-old, harmonica-playing brother.

> "Did you know? You're a genius." Andrew looked at her squarely, studied her face for a long moment. Finally he said, "I am not. I'm Andrew." His voice was very sure and he looked only faintly insulted at her name calling." (page 41, paperback edition)

He is certainly Andrew, and now he is Yolonda's genius. She is determined that the world will recognize his talent.

Just the Facts

LC 94-46962. 211p. 1995. $17.00 (ISBN 0-689-80001-0). Margaret K. McElderry Books.

Paperback. $4.99 (ISBN 0-689-81327-9). Aladdin.

Audio book. Unabridged, 5.25 hours. 1997. $18.99 (ISBN 0-553-47821-4). Bantam Doubleday Dell Audio.

Genres: contemporary realistic fiction, multicultural

Themes: music--blues, brothers and sisters, moving, school, friendship, child prodigy, African Americans, reading, violence, drugs, single parent families, harmonicas, urban life, teasing, self-image, self-reliance, peer relationships, responsibility, truth, aunts

Readability: Sixth grade

Interest Level: Fourth through seventh grade

Review Citations:

Horn Book Magazine 71(5):598 Sept/Oct 1995

Publishers Weekly 242(25):61 June 19, 1995

School Library Journal 41(7):76 July 1995

Curriculum Connections

Music (Blues, Harmonica)

Andrew has a special ability to express himself through the blues he blows on his harmonica. Provide students with information about this original American music. Books include *Blues for Dummies* by Lonnie Baker Brooks (IDG, 1998) and *Learn to Play Blues* by Anthony Marks and Howard Rye (Educational Development Center, 1995).

Play and/or make available a variety of recordings by legendary blues musicians such as B.B. King, Chuck Berry, Aretha Franklin, Bo Diddly, Howlin' Wolf, Muddy Waters, Koko Taylor, the Rolling Stones, Led Zeppelin, the Blues Brothers, and the Grateful Dead. Jazz complications of note include *The Golden Age of Blue Chicago* (Blue Chicago, 1998); *The Red Hot Mamas* (Blue Chicago, 1997); and *Clark Street Ramblers* (Blue Chicago, 1997). An excellent guide is *All Music Guide to the Blues: The Experts' Guide to the Best Blues Recordings* (2nd ed.) edited by Michael Erlewine, Chris Woodstra, Cub Koda, and Vladimir Bogdanov (Miller Freeman, 1999).

Related Websites

Introduction to Blues
   www.surfline.ne.jp/bear/introe.html

A Guide Through the Culture of the Blues
   www.yale.edu/ynhti/curriculum/units/1997/5/97.05.11.x.html

Jack's Harmonica Heaven
   www.volcano.net/~jackmearl/

Music for the New Age: Hohner, Inc.
   www.hohnerusa.com/

Social Issues (Drugs, Pushers, Role Playing)

After Andrew, Yolonda's young brother, comes home with a packet containing illegal drugs, their mother is determined to leave the city. Discuss the types of individuals who might sell drugs and why it would be to their advantage to give drugs to kids such as they gave to Andrew. Have students role play different situations where they are confronted with those who pressure them to use drugs. The picture book *The House That Crack Built* by Clark Taylor (Chronicle, 1992) and the publisher's website listed below with its numerous discussion ideas, links, and more, is an excellent place to begin.

Related Websites

The House that Crack Built
   www.chronbooks.com/Kids/Newsviews/Guides/Guide6/index.html

National Clearinghouse for Alcohol and Drug Information
   www.health.org/pubs/drugamer/drugamer.htm

Indiana Prevention Resource Center: Drug Information Menu
   www.drugs.indiana.edu/druginfo/home.html

Social Issues (School Violence, Guns)

Yolonda's mother wants to move her children out of Chicago because she is worried about violence at their school. She isn't the only one. Help students examine the tragic and painfully real problem of kids, guns, violence, and gun control with thought-provoking books like the following: the picture book *Just One Flick of a Finger* by Marybeth Lorbiecki (Dial, 1996); *Making Up Megaboy* by Virginia Walters (DK, 1998); *Twelve Shots: Outstanding Short Stories about Guns* by Harry Mazer (Delacorte, 1997); *Home Wars* by Dorothy R. Miller (Simon & Schuster, 1997); Walter Dean Myers' *Scorpions* (Harper, 1988); and Sonia Levitin's *Adam's War* (Dial, 1994).

Related Websites

National Center for Educational Statistics Report: Indicators of School Crime and Safety, 1999
   http://nces.ed.gov/pubsearch/pubsinfo.asp?pubid=1999057

U.S. Department of Justice: Building Blocks for Safe and Healthy Communities
   www.ojp.usdoj.gov/tree/

Gun Background Basics
   www.childrensdefense.org/youthviolence/gunbackground.html

Kids and Guns – Coordinating Committee on Gun Violence
   www.abanet.org/gunviol/youth.html

Keep on Reading

Chicago Blues by Julie Reece Deaver (HarperCollins, 1995). Lissa, a talented student at a Chicago arts college, raises her younger sister.

Attaboy, Sam! by Lois Lowry (Houghton Mifflin, 1992). Precocious four-year-old Sam and his family make imaginative presents for his mother's birthday.

The Facts and Fictions of Minna Pratt by Patricia MacLachlan (HarperCollins, 1988). Eleven-year-old Minna is a talented cello player and a great older sister to McGrew who hums headlines.

Junebug by Alice Mead (Farrar, Straus & Giroux, 1995). Living in the projects, Junebug takes care of his little sister, avoids the gangs of older boys, and daydreams about his future.

The Kid in the Red Jacket by Barbara Park (Knopf, 1987). From ten-year-old Howard Jeeter's perspective, his family's move from Arizona to Massachusetts is destroying his life.

Come Sing, Jimmy Jo by Katherine Paterson (Lodestar, 1985). A shy eleven year old from the Appalachian Mountains, Jimmy struggles with family jealousies, sudden fame, and upsetting knowledge about his father.

1996
HONOR

The Great Fire
Jim Murphy

Plot Summary

Through personal accounts, readers experience the fire that raged for 31 hours, destroying Chicago in 1871, leaving more than a hundred thousand people homeless.

Tips

An introduction, seven chapters, bibliography, source notes, and an index comprise this book. The fascinating text is interspersed with historical photographs and a series of maps that depict the advancing fire and the struggling citizens of Chicago.

Related Tips

The Great Fire Guide by Jim Murphy (Scholastic, 1997)

Author Information

Jim Murphy had a normal childhood in New Jersey. He played ball, walked railroad tracks, explored abandoned buildings, and was as mischievous as possible. He wasn't an avid reader until he was forbidden as a high school student to read *A Farewell to Arms* by Hemingway. That incident inspired him to begin reading and writing. Murphy worked for Clarion for seven years and then decided his earlier adventures would make interesting books for children—both fiction and nonfiction.

The Great Conflagration by James Washington Sheahan (Union Publishing, 1871) was the first book published about the Chicago fire, and it contained numerous recollections and interesting personal histories about the disaster. Reading this inspired Murphy to learn more and write his own version for children.

Related Author Resources

www.scils.rutgers.edu/special/kay/murphy.html

Book Clip

Mistakes and human error were to blame for the great Chicago fire in 1871. When the fire began, William Lee, a neighbor who lived down the street from the O'Leary's …

> … ran the three blocks to Bruno Goll's drugstore, determined to do what no one else in the neighborhood had thought about doing; turn in a fire alarm. At this point, the fire was barely fifteen minutes old. What followed was a series of fatal errors that set the fire free and doomed the city to a fiery death. (page 23, hardback edition)

Just the Facts

LC 94-9963 144p. 1995. $16.95 (ISBN 0-590-47167-4). Scholastic.

Audio book. Unabridged, 3 hours. 1998. $27 (ISBN 0-788-72077-5). Recorded books.

Genre: nonfiction

Themes: fires, Chicago fire (1871), disasters, courage, panic, homelessness, social classes, urban life —19th century, perseverance, relief society, myths, looting, riots, rebuilding, preservation, architecture

Readability: Seventh grade

Interest Level: Fifth through ninth grade

Review Citations:

Booklist 91(19-20):1757 June 1, 1995

Bulletin of the Center for Children's Books 48(9):297 May 1995

Horn Book Magazine 71(3):343 May/June 1995

Publishers Weekly 242(19):297 May 8, 1995

School Library Journal 41(7):89 July 1995

Curriculum Connections

History (Current Events, Disasters, Accidents)

Ask students to think about disasters in the United States—past and present—and understand the differences between a natural disaster versus human-caused disasters. Consider such events as the San Francisco earthquakes of 1906 and 1989, the Chicago fire of 1871, the Galveston hurricane of 1900, the Oklahoma bombing 1995, the Johnstown floods in 1889 and 1977, and so forth. Students can search for further information to learn more about these dramatic, high-interest events.

For further study about the Chicago fire, consult the following: *The Great Chicago Fire* by Robert Cromie (Rutledge Hill, 1993) and *Fire Disasters* by Rob Alcraft (Heinemann, 1999).

Related Websites

The Chicago Fire
www.chicagohs.org/history/fire.html

Chicago Public Library: 1871 The Great Fire
http://cpl.lib.uic.edu/004chicago/timeline/greatfire.html

Safety (Fire Prevention, Building Codes, Building Materials, Architecture, Emergency Plans)

Chicago residents learned after the fire that many buildings became firetraps because of the materials used in construction and the building designs. After the fire, building codes were created to prevent future disasters. Have students investigate local building and fire codes and the emergency disaster plan for your community. To make this more relevant, students can review, and perhaps make suggestions for changing your school's emergency plan.

Related Websites

Fire Prevention History
http://firesafety.buffnet.net/history.htm

Stanford University: *It's Academic – Disaster Preparedness for Schools* Video
www.stanford.edu/dept/EHS/train/video/online/index.html

Current Events (Chicago, Cows and Bulls, History, Public Art)

Use the unifying theme of cows (and bulls) to explore Chicago's past and present. Dividing into groups, students can learn more about these topics: the truth about Mrs. O'Leary's cow and the Chicago fire, the famous Chicago stockyards, the Chicago Bulls basketball team, and the public art cow exhibit which began in 1999. Use Upton Sinclair's turn-of-the-century novel exposing the terrible conditions of the stockyards, *The Jungle* (Bantam, 1981), and the related websites below for further information.

Related Websites

The O'Leary Legend
www.chicagohistory.org/fire/oleary/index.html

The Stockyards
www.chicagohistory.org/history/bibli.html

The Chicago Stock Yards on the Eve of the CIO (1936)
www.kentlaw.edu/ilhs/stkyards.html

Stock Yards of Chicago
http://stockyards.com/

Chicago Bulls
www.nba.com/bulls/

Cows on Parade in Chicago
http://geography.about.com/education/geography/library/weekly/aa080299.htm

Art Cows Chicago
www.cowsonparade.webjump.com/

Keep on Reading

Fire in Their Eyes: Wildfires and the People Who Fight Them by Karen Magnuson Beil (Harcourt Brace, 1999). Brave and skilled firefighters risk their lives battling fires in the wilderness.

Disaster by Richard Bonson (DK, 1997). Historical disasters across the world are presented on double-page spreads.

Flash Fire by Caroline B. Cooney (Scholastic, 1995). The fire in the narrow canyon is terrifying and unpredictable, and the children have to save themselves.

Survival! Fire (Chicago, 1871) by Kathleen Duey (Aladdin, 1998). Nate looks desperately for family members as the Chicago fire rages.

Catching Fire: The Story of Firefighting by Gena K. Gorrell (Tundra, 1999). This nonfiction view of firefighting provides information on wildfires, animal rescues, and more.

Children of the Fire by Harriette Gillem Robinet (Atheneum, 1991). Eleven-year-old Hallelujah experiences the historic Chicago fire.

1997

MEDAL

The View from Saturday
E. L. Konigsburg

Plot Summary

By chance and fate, four gifted sixth graders (Noah, Nadia, Ethan and Julian) become "The Souls" and take their Academic Bowl Team to the state finals. Their personal stories and relationship with Mrs. Olinski, their inspiring teacher, give them each a unique edge.

Tips

While the numerous characters and frequent flashbacks may confuse and discourage some readers, this sophisticated story with alternating narratives will appeal to good readers. To introduce the book and some of the characters, read aloud the first chapter and the first four sections of the second chapter (through page 24, hardback edition).

Related Tips

The View from Saturday by E. L. Konigsburg (Scholastic, 1999)

http://207.237.120.51/disc/view_from_saturday.html

Author Information

E(laine) L(obl) Konigsburg grew up in Pennsylvania. She read extensively as a child but felt the books she read "told her nothing about the world in which I was living." While a chemistry major at Carnegie Mellon University, Konigsburg learned to write clearly and concisely, and later as a science teacher, she learned to be specific and "ask big questions." Claiming she "had a mind for chemistry, but not the temperament," Konigsburg began writing when her youngest child entered school. Retaining the ability to see herself as the center of the universe (like children do), Konigsburg writes eloquently for children who ask questions and seek answers.

Related Author Resources

Talk Talk: A Children's Book Author Speaks to Grown-Ups by E. L. Konigsburg (Atheneum, 1995).

Video: *Good Conversation! A Talk with E. L. Konigsburg.* Color, 22 min. (Tim Podell Productions, 1995).

www.randomhouse.com/teachers/authors/koni.html

http://slis-two.lis.fsu.edu/~5340f/bio.html

http://scrtec.org/track/tracks/t00401.html

www.indiana.edu/~eric_rec/ieo/bibs/konigs.htm

Newbery Acceptance Speech: *Horn Book Magazine* 73(4):404 Jul/Aug 1997

Just the Facts

LC 95-52624. 163p. 1996. $16 (ISBN 0-689-80993-X). Atheneum.

Paperback. $4.50 (ISBN 0-689-81721-5). Aladdin.

Audio book. Unabridged, 4 hrs., 47 min. $23.98 (ISBN 0-8072-7890 4). Listening Library.

Genres: contemporary realistic fiction, multicultural

Themes: friendship, gifted students, teamwork, school life, teacher/student relationships, physical handicaps, contests, weddings, divorce, grandparents, sea turtles, civility, inclusiveness, animal conservation, Random Acts of Kindness, acronyms, magic, dogs, theater, environment, Yiddish

Readability: Upper sixth grade

Interest Level: Fifth through eighth grade

Review Citations:

Booklist 93(4):424 Oct 15, 1996

Bulletin of the Center for Children's Books 50(3):103 Nov 1996

Horn Book Magazine 78(1):60 Jan/Feb 1997

Publishers Weekly 243(3):242 July 22, 1996

School Library Journal 42(9):204 Sept 1996

Book Clip

It's Bowl Day, the academic contest begins as the Commissioner of Education draws the first question for Mrs. Olinski's sixth grade team.

> He withdrew a piece of paper, unfolded it, and read, "What is the meaning of the word *calligraphy* and from what language does it derive?" A buzzer sounded. Mrs. Olinski knew whose it was. She was sure of it. She leaned back and relaxed. She was not nervous. Excited, yes. Nervous, no. The television lights glanced off Noah Gershom's glasses. He had been the first chosen. (pages 3-4, hardback edition)

And so it begins—the story of The Souls—and their own particular *View from Saturday*.

Curriculum Connections

Art (Calligraphy, Illuminated Manuscripts)

The first question posed at the Bowl concerns calligraphy. Fortunately, Noah Gershom has experience with this art form. Provide your students with examples of illuminated letters such as those in Jonathan Hunt's *Illuminations* (Bradbury, 1989) and Elizabeth B. Wilson's *Bibles and Bestiaries: A Guide to Illuminated Manuscripts* (Farrar, Straus & Giroux, 1994). Show students Karen Brookfield's *Book* (Knopf, 1993) and invite a calligrapher to share their materials and give beginning instruction. As a final activity students can create invitations to a class party or other special event.

Related Websites

The On-Line Calligraphy Lesson
   www.riverflow.com/calligraphy/lesson.htm

Blackletter Alphabets
   www.catalog.com/gallery/Gothicx.html

Chinese Calligraphy: Language as Art
   http://tqjunior.advanced.org/3614/Default.htm

Appreciation of The Art of Chinese Calligraphy
   www.chinapage.org/calligraphy.html

Language Arts (Acronyms, Dictionaries, Research)

One of the questions posed at the Academic Bowl was about acronyms. Share some examples of acronyms such as NOW (National Organization for Women) and NASA (National Aeronautics and Space Administration). Then hold a contest among groups of students to see how many acronyms each can find and highlight in a week of newspapers. Have groups compile their list of acronyms, along with the meanings. The group with the most acronyms wins. For extra credit, challenge students to create their own acronyms for real or imaginary organizations.

Related Websites

The WorldWideWeb Acronym and Abbreviation Server
   www.ucc.ie/info/net/acronyms/acro.html

Derivatives Acronyms
   www.numa.com/ref/acronym.htm

Science (Sea Turtles, Endangered Species, Research)

Nadia's grandfather and his wife work hard as volunteers helping to preserve endangered sea turtles. Use the following references for further research: *Biology and Conservation of Sea Turtles* by Karen A. Bjorndal (Smithsonian, 1995); *Into the Sea* by Alix Berenzy and Brenda Z. Guiberson (Henry Holt, 1996); *Sea Turtles* by Emilie U. Lepthien (Children's Press, 1997); and *Sea Turtles* by Jeff Ripple (Voyageur, 1996).

Related Websites

Turtle Trax
   www.turtles.org

Marine Turtle Newsletter
   www.seaturtle.org/mtn/

Sea World: Sea Turtles
   www.seaworld.org/Sea_Turtle/seaturtle.html

Keep on Reading

Can't Catch Me, I'm the Gingerbread Man by Jamie Gilson (Beech Tree, 1997). Mitch enters a bake-off contest to save his family's business.

The Million Dollar Shot by Dan Gutman (Hyperion, 1998). After winning a poetry contest, Eddie Balls has a chance to score a million dollars at the NBA finals.

The Great Toilet Paper Caper by Gary Hogg (Little Apple, 1997). The whole town becomes involved with Spencer as he tries to break the record for the world's largest toilet-paper roll.

The Exiles by Hilary McKay (Margaret McElderry, 1992). Sent to spend the summer with their grandmother, the four Conroy sisters become involved in hilarious adventures.

Oh No, It's Robert by Barbara Seuling (Front Street, 1999). Robert struggles to win a student achievement contest.

The Library Card by Jerry Spinelli (Apple, 1998). Four separate stories feature a magic library card that helps each young character.

1997
HONOR

A Girl Named Disaster
Nancy Farmer

Plot Summary

Nhamo (the girl named "Disaster") is encouraged by her loyal grandmother to run away from their Mozambique village and the cruel arranged marriage. Setting off for Zimbabwe (and freedom), Nhamo depends on the spirit world and her own courage and resourcefulness to help her survive.

Tips

The forty-two chapters can be grouped in three parts: chapters one through twelve describe Nhamo's life in her traditional village; chapters thirteen through thirty-one follow her journey; and chapters thirty-two through forty-two describe her life in Zimbabwe. Preceding the novel is a cast of characters and three maps. At the end is a glossary, "The History and Peoples of Zimbabwe and Mozambique," "The Belief System of the Shona," and a bibliography.

Author Information

Born in Arizona, Nancy Farmer attended the University of California and worked as a lab technician in Berkeley.

Her varied careers include joining the Peace Corps and going to India, and working as a chemist and entomologist in Zimbabwe where she met her husband. Farmer lived in Africa for seventeen years and says her experiences there had a major effect on her writing. She grew up surrounded by storytelling and is now a professional storyteller. Her rules for becoming a successful writer are: "(1) Read as much as possible, (2) Write as much as possible for several years, and (3) Submit manuscripts to a wide variety of editors." Farmer now lives with her family in California.

Book Clip

While trying to survive and reach freedom in Zimbabwe, Nhamo is hiding on a narrow ledge by the mouth of a cave when she is challenged by a fierce baboon troop.

> They found the cook-fire and stopped short. Nhamo held her breath. A large male shouted a challenge. His eyes flashed white and his big fangs yawned. The message was perfectly clear: *Come out, whoever you are, so I can rip you to shreds!* (page 156, hardback and paperback edition)

Just the Facts

LC 97-28173 309p. 1996. $19.95 (ISBN 0-531-09539-8). Orchard.

Paperback. $4.99 (ISBN 0-14-038635-1). Puffin.

Audio book. Unabridged, 12.25 hours. 1998. $75 (ISBN 0-788-71342-6). Recorded Books.

Genres: adventure, contemporary realistic fiction, multicultural

Themes: heroines, survival, grandmothers, arranged marriages, superstitions, storytelling, Africa, freedom, independence, customs, diversity, cholera, loneliness, fear, observation, rites-of passage, totems, baboons, revenge, hunger, dreams

Readability: Seventh grade

Interest Level: Sixth through twelfth grade

Review Citations:

Booklist 93(1):118 Sept 1, 1996

Bulletin of the Center for Children's Books 50(4):133 Dec 1996

English Journal 86(7):124 Nov 1997

Horn Book Magazine 72(6):734 Nov/Dec 1996

Publishers Weekly 243(44):82 Oct 28, 1996

School Library Journal 42(10):144 Oct 1996

When translated Nhamo's name means "disaster." Does this mean her journey (and life) will end in disaster?

Curriculum Connections

Current Events (Landmines, Research, War, History, Detection, Humanitarian Projects)

While Nhamo is sneaking across the border to Zimbabwe, she sees an elephant blown up by a landmine. Landmines have been used in warfare for the past century, however, even when the wars are over, landmines remain as a hidden enemy. Some kill and maim soon after the war, others lie in wait for generations. Using Internet and print sources, students can find out more about the global movement (and the U.S. government's position) to ban landmines, the Nobel Peace Prize awarded to Jody Williams in 1997, and the current efforts to detect and remove landmines.

Related Websites

Clearing the Killing Fields: New Technologies for Land Mine Detection Aim at 2010 Goal
http://abcnews.go.com/sections/tech/DailyNews/landmines990305.html

Landmines – Links
http://etro.vub.ac.be/minedet/links.html

Internet Online Petition to Ban Landmines Worldwide
www.demon.co.uk/aesop/landm4.htm

Literature (African Folktales, Storytelling, Picture Books)

Nhamo is a master at storytelling, often drawing upon the rich traditions of her culture as well as her imagination and circumstances. Provide a classroom library of exquisitely told African folktales found in collections and as picture books. Be sure to include some of the following: Lloyd Alexander's *The Fortune-Tellers* (Dutton, 1992); David L. Anderson's *The Origin of Life on Earth: An African Creation Myth* (Sights Productions, 1991); Gerald McDermott's *Zomo the Rabbit: A Trickster Tale from West Africa* (Harcourt, Brace Jovanovich, 1992); Tololwa M. Mollel's *The Orphan Boy* (Clarion, 1990); Judy Sierra's *The Elephant's Wrestling Match* (Dutton, 1992); Leo and Diane Dillon's *Why Mosquitoes Buzz in People's Ears: A West African Tale* (Dial, 1975); John Steptoe's *Mufaro's Beautiful Daughters: An African Tale* (Lothrop, 1987); and David Wisniewski's *Lion King of Mali* (Houghton Mifflin, 1992).

Science (Baboons, Primates, Research)

Nhamo's experiences with the baboon troop illustrate how human-like many of their characteristics are. Study more about baboons using the following resources: *Almost Human: A Journey into the World of Baboons* by Shirley C. Strum (Norton, 1990) and *In Quest of the Sacred Baboon: A Scientist's Journey* by Hans Kummer (Princeton University Press, 1995).

Related Websites

Anthropologist Finds Another Link between Humans and Other Primates
www.wm.edu/wmnews/research/monkeys.html

International Wildlife Magazine: Moving the Pumphouse Gang
www.nwf.org/nwf/intlwild/1998/baboon.html

Stanford Today Online – Essay: "A Baboon's Life"
www.stanford.edu/dept/news/stanfordtoday/ed/9607/9607essy01.shtml

The Baboon
www.ixpres.com/netjert/baboon.htm

Keep on Reading

The Storyteller's Beads by Jane Kurtz (Gulliver Books, 1998). While on a dangerous journey, two young Ethiopian girls overcome their cultural differences.

Thunder Cave by Roland Smith (Hyperion, 1995). Following his mother's death, fourteen-year-old Jake runs away to Kenya to find his father, a wildlife biologist.

Shabanu, Daughter of the Wind by Suzanne Fisher Staples (Random House, 1989). Independent and free-spirited, eleven-year-old Shabanu is resistant to the idea of an arranged marriage, especially to settle a feud.

The Bedouin's Gazelle by Frances Temple (Orchard, 1996). Set in the fourteenth century, this tale is about Bedouin cousins who are betrothed at birth.

Grab Hands and Run by Frances Temple (Orchard, 1993). Fearing for their lives, twelve-year-old Felipe, his younger sister, and their mother flee El Salvador for Canada.

I Rode a Horse of Milk White Jade by Diane Lee Wilson (Orchard, 1998). A strong-willed Chinese girl has adventures in the time of Kublai Khan.

1997
HONOR
The Moorchild
Eloise McGraw

Plot Summary

Saaski is considered "freaky-odd" by the other children in the village, and is taunted and teased endlessly. She's actually a changeling—half fairy and half human—and at home in neither world. Saaski loves her mum and da in her own way and finds some peace playing the pipes and learning about healing from her grandmother. But when the villagers decide to persecute Saaski and her family, she acts on previously unknown courage to travel back to the mound and rescue her parents' real child.

Tips

The twenty-four chapters, divided into five parts, are preceded by two definitions of a "changeling." Fantasy fans will be the readers most enchanted with this book.

Author Information

Eloise McGraw was born in Texas and grew up in Oklahoma. Her first short story was written when she was eight years old and she kept on writing until she was twenty, when she decided to be an artist. She tried that for ten years but then re-discovered her true vocation when she sold a short story to a children's magazine. Throughout the past five decades McGraw has steadily written and published award-winning books. Her creative process begins with a well-defined character and then the plot evolves. McGraw and her husband (children's author William Corbin) have lived in Oregon since 1953. *The Moorchild* is McGraw's twentieth book.

Book Clip

Living in a place where humans believe in fairy folks, Saaski always feels caught between two worlds and has never known why. She...

> ... was silent, her skin deliciously crawling. A phrase echoed somewhere in the depths of her mind: *Time runs different in the Mound.* Someone had said that once—she could almost hear the voice. But it could have been anybody. She had heard numberless stories about the Folk and their tricks and their hidden homeland somewhere inside the hills .... Strange things happened; everyone knew they did. And some were past explaining. (page 117, paperback edition)

Just the Facts

LC 95-34107 240p. 1996. $16 (ISBN 0-689-80654-X). Margaret K. McElderry.

Paperback. 256p. 1998. $4.50 (ISBN 0-689-83022-X). Aladdin Books.

Audio book. Unabridged, 6 hours. 1998. $25 (ISBN 0-788-71920-3). Recorded Books.

Genre: fantasy

Themes: changelings, fate, banishment, fairies, home, adjustment, survival, superstitions, belonging, individuality, rumors, reading, writing, friendship, bagpipes, runes, herbs, curiosity, fear, ridicule, plagues, gypsies, talent

Readability: Seventh grade

Interest Level: Fourth through seventh grade

Review Citations:

Booklist 92(13):436 Mar 1, 1996

Bulletin of the Center for Children's Books 49(11):345 June 1996

Horn Book Magazine 72(5):598 Sept/Oct 1996

Publishers Weekly 243(15):69 Apr 8, 1996

School Library Journal 42(4):136 Apr 1996

Saaski feels more at home by herself on the moor than in the village with the other children—is that past explaining too?

Curriculum Connections

Literature (Dedications, Books)

Most authors dedicate their books to a specific person or group of people. Some dedicate books to their readers: In *The Moorchild* Eloise McGraw wrote, "To all children who have ever felt different," and Lois Lowry dedicated *The Giver*, "For all the children to whom we entrust the future." Have your students collect a variety of dedications from all sorts of books. Students who scour the library shelves looking for interesting dedications will be handling potential reading experiences. Encourage students to collect the most interesting (or unusual) dedications they find and create a display or bulletin board.

Research (Sociology, Biology, Ethics, Interviews, Opinions, Discussion)

Saaski is half fairy and half human, and even though she tries, behaving like a human is nearly impossible for her. She's never quite sure how she is different. The answer to the question "What does it mean to be human?" is sought by individuals in daily life and in many disciplines—anthropology, biology, religion, and so forth.

Divide your students into research groups to search print and Internet resources; interview peers and adults; and examine literature, poetry, and quotations to develop their lists or criteria to answer this question. Create a "What does it mean to be human?" display featuring the diversity of answers and thoughts students are sure to collect.

Literature (Biracial, Multi-ethnic, Sociology, Children, Families)

Like Saaski, many biracial or multi-ethnic children may feel as though they fit into no particular culture. Along with a study of multiculturalism, encourage students to discover the realities of belonging to two or more cultures. Provide some of the following books which feature characters who are either biracial or multi-ethnic, and often struggle to fit in: *The Color of Water: A Black Man's Tribute to His White Mother* by James McBride (Riverhead, 1996); *The Window* by Michael Dorris (Disney, 1997); *Zack* by William Bell (Simon & Schuster, 1999); *The Last Rainmaker* by Sherry Garland (Harcourt Brace, 1997); and *Sun Dance at Turtle Rock* by Patricia Costa Viglucci (Stone Pine Books, 1996).

Keep on Reading

The Fairy Rebel by Lynne Reid Banks (Camelot, 1989). A fairy grants two humans their wish to have a baby, and they all face the anger of the Fairy Queen.

The Folk Keeper by Franny Billingsley (Atheneum, 1999). Corinna, a folk keeper, protects the farm from the fierce and ravenous Folk who live beneath the land.

The Boggart by Susan Cooper (Margaret K. McElderry, 1993). The Volnik family inherits a Scottish castle, its antiques, and an ancient and mischievous spirit—the Boggart.

In the Same Place But Different by Perry Nodelman (Simon & Schuster, 1995). Andrea, Johnny Nesbit's baby sister, must be rescued from the fairies who have replaced her with a changeling.

Outside Over There by Maurice Sendak (HarperCollins, 1981). Young Idaho has to save her baby sister from the goblins who took her away.

The Fairies' Ring: A Book of Fairy Stories & Poems collected by Jane Yolen (Dutton, 1999). Fairly lore from all over the world are showcased in stories and poetry.

1997

HONOR

The Thief
Megan Whalen Turner

Plot Summary

Imprisoned for stealing, Gen can win his freedom by accompanying the magus and his apprentices on a quest to find and steal a legendary stone. It is believed the owner of this treasure will gain the power to rule the kingdom. Gen, charmingly egocentric, is a great thief and a loyal subject.

Tips

Following the twelve chapters of this fantasy is a brief author note indicating the relationship of this story to the Greek landscape and medieval events. The surprising twist of events at the conclusion will delight readers or listeners, and inspire them to read it again. Interspersed among the story are the creation myths told by the travelers—all set off in a different font beginning in chapter five.

Related Tips

http://home.att.net/~mwturner/ (See "Author's Note to *The Thief*" within the entry)

Author Information

Because her father was in the army, Megan Whalen Turner's family moved from place to place throughout her childhood. In fact, she never lived anywhere for more than three years until she attended college in Chicago. Turner considered writing as a career as early as fifth grade after she exhausted her reading sources and wanted to write her own great books. Now married to a research professor and the mother of two children, Turner still continues to move frequently. She uses these changes as opportunities to look for different story settings and landscapes.

Related Author Resources

http://home.att.net/~mwturner/

Book Clip

I was thinner than I had been when I was first arrested. The large iron ring around my waist had grown loose, but not loose enough to fit over the bones of my hips. Few prisoners wore chains in their cells, only those that the king particularly

Just the Facts

LC 95-41040. 219p. 1996. $15 (ISBN 0-688-14627-9). Greenwillow.

Paperback. 1998. $4.99 (ISBN 0-140-38834-6). Puffin.

Audio book. Unabridged, 7.5 hours. 1998. $44 (ISBN 0-7887-1346-9). Recorded Books.

Genres: fantasy, adventure

Themes: thieves, heroes, bragging, apprentices, freedom, treasures, royalty, scholars, journeys, horses, myths, politics, pride, prisons, plagues, immortality, mazes, premonitions, tolerance, cooperation, loyalty, religion

Readability: Sixth grade

Interest Level: Fifth through ninth grade

Review Citations:

Booklist 93(9-10):863 Jan 1, 1997

Bulletin of the Center for Children's Books 50(3):117 Nov 1996

Horn Book Magazine 72(6):747 Nov/Dec 1996

Publishers Weekly 243(43):84 Oct 21, 1996

School Library Journal 42(10):150 Oct 1996

disliked: counts or dukes or the minister of the exchequer when he told the king there wasn't any more money to spend. I was certainly none of those things, but I suppose it's safe to say that the king disliked me. (pages 1-2, hardback and paper back editions)

Yes, Gen, the king does dislike you. But you are the only one who can steal the legendary stone that will give him ultimate power beyond his kingdom … and give you your freedom.

Curriculum Connections

Careers (Apprenticeships, Internship)

Sophos and Ambiades are apprenticed to the magus—the powerful advisor to the king. Students of today can learn about other careers through guest speakers, School-to-Work programs, career days, internships, etc. Participation in Take Our Daughters to Work Day in April each year, which, in some areas, also includes participation by boys as well, is a great opportunity to provide students with specific job-related information.

Related websites

Office of Apprenticeship Training, Employer & Labor Service
   www.doleta.gov/atels_bat/

Take Our Daughters to Work Day
   www.ms.foundation.org/

National School-to-Work Learning Center
   www.stw.ed.gov/index.htm

Literature (Creation Myths, Creative Writing)

While they are traveling toward the stone the thief will steal, Gen and his fellow travelers entertain and educate themselves by re-telling creation stories specific to their culture. Nearly every culture explains their beginnings with stories like these. Create a classroom library of creation tales from around the world using the following books: *In the Beginning: Creation Stories from around the World* by Virginia Hamilton (Harcourt Brace Jovanovich, 1988); *Why There Is No Arguing in Heaven: A Mayan Myth* by Deborah Nourse Lattimore (Harper & Row, 1989); *The Origin of Life on Earth: An African Creation Myth* by David L. Anderson (Sights Productions, 1991); *All of You Was Singing* by Richard Lewis (Atheneum, 1991); *Primal Myths: Creation Myths around the World* by Barbara C. Sproul (Harper, 1992); *The Woman Who Fell from the Sky: The Iroquois Story of Creation* by John

Bierhorst (William Morrow, 1993); *The Story of the Creation: Words from Genesis* by Jane Ray (Dutton, 1993); and *A Dictionary of Creation Myths* by David Adams Leeming (Oxford University Press, 1996).

Students can compare and contrast creation stories, paying particular attention to similarities of character traits, events, use of power, and relationships between gods. Like Turner, students can then create original stories explaining mythological beginnings.

Related websites

Creation Myths--Research lesson
   www.learningspace.org/instruct/lplan/library/Wolfe.html

Literature (Writing, Reference Books, Organization)

Working in groups students can create a "Reader's Reference Guide" to *The Thief*. Include a character identification list (noting relationships), a guide to the myths, a glossary defining unique words, a detailed map, a traveler's guide which would include places to visit and accommodations available, etc. Chart the traveler's journey on the map, noting travel time and highlighting where significant events occurred. Be sure to keep a copy of this guide along with *The Thief* for future readers.

Keep on Reading:

The King's Shadow by Elizabeth Adler (Bantam, 1997). A young Welsh serf dreams of becoming a storyteller to express his loyalty to his king.

The Iron Ring by Lloyd Alexander (Dutton, 1997). Tamar, a young king in ancient India, journeys to a distant kingdom to settle a debt of honor.

The Shakespeare Stealer by Gary Blackwood (Dutton, 1998). An orphan with the ability to write a unique short-hand code is ordered to infiltrate the Globe Theatre and write down Shakespeare's plays.

Tusk and Stone by Malcolm Bosse (Front Street, 1995). Taken prisoner and forced into slavery, young Arjun becomes a master stonecarver.

Ghost in the Tokaido Inn by Dorothy Hoobler (Philomel, 1999). Fourteen-year-old Seikei risks his life by speaking out to defend a young girl who has stolen a precious jewel.

Sabriel by Garth Nix (HarperCollins, 1996). Determined to find her magician father, Sabriel journeys through the Old Kingdom and faces enemies.

1997 HONOR

Belle Prater's Boy
Ruth White

Plot Summary

Twelve-year-old Gypsy tells the story of Belle Prater's boy, Woodrow, who moves in next door with their grandparents. The town is abuzz wondering about the sudden disappearance of Woodrow's mother. Gypsy and Woodrow become fast and loyal friends as they help each other deal with family secrets.

Tips

Regional slang makes this a good book for independent reading. The relationships, stories, jokes, and slight suspense are all elements readers will appreciate.

Related Tips

www.randomhouse.com/teachers/guides/bell.html

Author Information

Ruth White grew up poor in a Virginia coal mine town. She loved playing in the creeks and fondly remembers family read-alouds. White knew she would someday be a writer even before she started school and she now uses her memories of childhood abundantly in her books.

Attending college offered White the opportunity to teach, become a school librarian, and finally to write.

Related Author Resources

www.randomhouse.com/teachers/guides/rwhi.html
www.carr.lib.md.us/authco/white.htm

Book Clip

When Woodrow, Belle Prater's boy, comes to live next door to his cousin, Gypsy, a wonderful friendship develops.

> "This is the day I will choose," Woodrow said softly. "Choose for what?" I said, and yawned. I was about ready to turn in. "Mama told me when we die, we're allowed to live one day over again—just one—exactly as it was. This is the day I will choose." I was surprised. A day that for me had been only slightly special was the most wonderful day of his life. It made me wonder how bad things had been in Crooked Ridge. (page 37-38, hardback edition)

Belle Prater has vanished, and Gypsy is slowly learning

Just the Facts

LC 94-43625. 196p. 1996. $16 (ISBN 0-374-30668-0). Farrar, Straus & Giroux.
Paperback. 1998. $3.99 (ISBN 0-440-41372-9). Yearling.
Audio book. Unabridged, 3.5 hours. $19.99 (ISBN 0-553-478-982). Bantam Doubleday Dell Audio.

Genres: historical fiction, humor

Themes: families, truth, death, disappearances, cousins, grandparents, sisters, friendship, secrets, identity, coping, rural life, poetry, nightmares, step parenting, eyes, storytelling, suicide, superstitions, Appalachia

Readability: Fifth grade
Interest Level: Fourth through ninth grade
Review Citations:
Booklist 92(16):1434 Apr 15, 1996
Bulletin of the Center for Children's Books 49(8):281 Apr 1996
Horn Book Magazine 72(5):601 Sept/Oct 1996
Publisher's Weekly 245(6):26 Feb 9, 1998
School Library Journal 42(4):158 Apr 1996

the secrets that surround Belle's disappearance and her own recurring nightmare.

Curriculum Connections

Economics (Inflation, Consumer Price Index, Food Prices, History)

Belle Prater's Boy is set in 1953. The world, including prices, has changed a lot since then. Have students create a shopping list (for groceries, clothes, haircuts, comic books and holiday gifts) using the information about prices featured in the book. Also glean information from magazines and newspapers published in 1953. After compiling the shopping list, students can then complete the project by researching similar products and discovering their current costs using the websites below. Further price comparisons can include the current global economy.

Related Websites

The Dismal Scientist: Inflation and the Time Value of Money – CPI Calculator
www.dismal.com/toolbox/cpi_index.stm

Consumer Price Index, 1950–1997
http://nutmeg.ctstateu.edu/personal/faculty/pocock/CPI.htm

Literature/Contests

Belle Prater's Boy has a great opening line. Have students search for other books with wonderful first sentences and record them on file cards along with the title and author. Create a ballot and have the students vote for their five favorites. Feature the top vote getting books in your classroom or library.

Related Websites

First Lines
www.people.cornell.edu/pages/jad22/

Science (Anatomy, Eyes, Near Sightedness, Dissection)

By the story's end, arrangements have been made for Woodrow to have eye surgery on his crossed eyes. Looking at the inside of the eye can provide a fascinating study; help satisfy this curiosity with the following Internet resources.

Related Websites

Anatomy of an Eye
www.lasersite.com/Anatomy/index.htm

How the Eye Works
www.lasersite.com/Eyeworks/index.htm

The Exploratorium: Cow's Eye Dissection
www.exploratorium.edu/learning_studio/cow_eye/index.html

Eyes Eyes Eyes
www.internz.com/walton/Room2/Eyes/eye.html

Keep on Reading

My Louisiana Sky by Kimberly Holt (Henry Holt, 1998). Set in Louisiana in the 1950s, this story centers on Tiger Ann and her relationship with her parents, grandmother, and aunt.

Rabble Starkey by Lois Lowry (Houghton Mifflin, 1987). Rabble and her mother move in with her best friend, Veronica, so Rabble's mother can care for them and Veronica's sick mother.

Journey by Patricia MacLachlan (Delacorte, 1991). After Journey's mother leaves him and his sister, they go to live with his grandparents.

Flip-Flop Girl by Katherine Paterson. (Dutton, 1994). An odd friendship develops between two lonely girls who have each lost their father.

Strays Like Us by Richard Peck (Dial, 1998). When her mother is unable to care for her, Molly is sent to live with her great-aunt Fay.

Return to Bitter Creek by Doris Buchanan Smith (Viking, 1988). Lacey has a difficult time adjusting when she and her mother move to live with their large extended family in southern Appalachia.

1998

MEDAL

Out of the Dust

Karen Hesse

Plot Summary

Life is bleak during the Oklahoma Dust Bowl days, and like many, Billie Jo and her parents are barely surviving on their farm. An accidental fire leaves Billie Jo's hands horribly burned and fatally injures her mother. The dust storms and poverty continue and Billie Jo's father is buried in grief and sorrow.

Tips

The free verse in *Out of the Dust*, as spare as the Oklahoma countryside, is divided by seasons. There are a number of ways to introduce this book—create posters by matching some of the dust bowl photographs on the Internet (see the art curriculum section below) with selected excerpts from the book; play ragtime music of that era so students can "hear" Billie Jo's piano playing; and/or read Margot Theis Raven' picture book, *Angels in the Dust* (BridgeWater, 1997).

Related Tips

Out of the Dust by Karen Hesse (Scholastic, 2000)

Author Information

Karen Hesse has been a teacher, librarian, secretary, typesetter, poet, and proofreader as well as a children's author. She grew up in Baltimore surrounded by people but often feeling isolated. Hesse says she was "thin and pasty" and even though she had friends, never felt she could trust anyone with her secrets. An avid reader, Hesse wishes more books about real issues had been available to her.

Out of the Dust was inspired by research Hesse was doing for another book when she discovered an old newspaper published in Oklahoma during the Dust Bowl era. The jacket cover is a Walker Evans photograph taken during the Depression and published originally in *Let Us Now Praise Famous Men* by James Agee (Houghton, rev. ed. 1989), a photograph/text documentary of the Great Depression. Hesse lives in Vermont with her husband and two daughters, and has written a memoir for Amy Ehrlich's *When I Was Your Age: Original Stories about Growing Up* (Candlewick, 1999).

Just the Facts

LC 96-40344. 240p. 1997 $15.95 (ISBN 0-590-36080-9). Scholastic.

Paperback. $4.99 (ISBN 0-590-37125-8). Scholastic.

Audio book. Unabridged, 2 hours. 1998. $15.95 (ISBN 0-8072-8050-X). Listening Library.

Genres: historical fiction, poetry

Themes: Great Depression, drought, 1930s, Oklahoma, Dust Bowl, families, farm life, accidents, fathers and daughters, grief, death, community, compassion, perseverance, fires, ecology, music, government, school life, health, skin cancer, free verse, prairie life

Readability: Fifth grade

Interest Level: Fifth grade and up

Review Citations:

Booklist 94(3):330 Oct 1, 1997

Bulletin of the Center for Children's Books 51(3):128 Dec 1997

English Journal 88(3):120 Jan 1999

Horn Book Magazine 74(1):73 Jan/Feb 1998

Publishers Weekly 244(35):72 Aug 25, 1997

School Library Journal 43(9):217 Sept 1997

Related Author Resources

www.riverdale.k12.or.us/~cmaxwell/hesse.htm (short!)

Newbery Acceptance speech: *Horn Book Magazine* 124(4):422 Jul/Aug 1998

Book Clip

It's the middle of the night on the Oklahoma plains. Lightning and wind wake Billie Jo.

> I sensed it before I knew it was coming.
> I heard it,
> smelled it,
> tasted it.
> Dust.
> …
> Daddy came in,
> He sat across from Ma and blew his nose.
> Mud streamed out.
> He coughed and spit out
> mud.
> If he had cried,
> his tears would have been mud too,
> but he didn't cry.
> And neither did Ma. (pages 31 & 33, paperback edition.)

By 1934, folks were nearly numb from the drought and the dust. It covered cattle, choked the plants, and affected everything. Billie Jo struggles to get *Out of the Dust.*

Curriculum Connections

Art (Photography, History, Great Depression)

The jacket photo, taken by famous photographer Walker Evans in 1930s, is part of the "Farm Security Administration" collection in the Library of Congress Prints and Photographs division. Thousands of black and white photographs from Walker Evans, Dorothea Lange and dozens of others artists who captured the Great Depression are available on the Internet.

The following books will also complement this area of study: *Dorothea Lange* by Robyn Montana Turner (Little Brown, 1994); *Restless Spirit: The Life and Work of Dorothea Lange* by Elizabeth Partridge (Viking, 1998); and *Photographers: History and Culture through the Camera* (American Profiles) by Nancy Jackson (Facts on File, 1997). Cynthia Rylant paid tribute to Walker Evans in her evocative book of poetry *Something Permanent* (Harcourt, 1994).

Related Websites

America from the Great Depression to World War II: Black and White Photographs from the FSA-OWI 1935–1945 (Note: Browse or search by subject, creator and/or by state and county. In the subject index, the 44 photographs of "Dust Storm – Oklahoma" will be of particular interest.)

http://rs6.loc.gov/ammen/fsahtm/fahome.html

Walker Evans Project

http://memory.loc.gov/ammem/fsahtml/fahome.html

Dorothea Lange Archive--Oakland Museum of California

www.museumca.org/global/art/collections_dorothea_lange.html

Economics (History, Inflation, Home Economics, Consumer Price Index)

Billie bought the ingredients for a birthday cake for about 50 cents (page 17, paperback edition). Have your students figure out what ingredients were required for a cake at that time (consult a 1930s cookbook), what it would cost today to bake that cake, and then what each of those ingredients would have cost in 1934. As an extension, students can also chart other historical comparisons with the following resources.

Related Websites

Then and Now: Prices

http://gopher.sos.state.mi.us/history/museum/kidstuff/depressn/costlist.html

The Dismal Scientist: Inflation and the Time Value of Money - CPI Calculator

www.dismal.com/toolbox/cpi_index.stm

Consumer Price Index, 1950-1997

http://nutmeg.ctstateu.edu/personal/faculty/pocock/CPI.htm

History (Dust Bowl, Great Depression)

The following nonfiction books and websites complement and enhance what students can learn about this period of history. Provide Jerry Stanley's *Children of the Dust Bowl: The True Story of the School at Weedpatch* (Crown, 1992) which uses interviews, documents and period photographs to tell of the stories of children of farm families who moved to California from Oklahoma to escape the dust storms as well as *The Dust Bowl: Disaster on the Plains* by Tricia Andryszewski (Millbrook, 1994). Strengthen the use of these books with the "America from the Great Depression to World War II: Black and White Photographs from the FSA-OWI

1935–1945" website in the Art curriculum suggestion.

Angels in the Dust, a picture book by Margot Theis Raven and illustrated by Roger Essley (BridgeWater, 1997), is based on a true story of a family struggling with the drought and winds on a Dust Bowl farm. Reading it aloud will prove excellent for introducing *Out of the Dust* or for stimulating discussions about the common events in both books.

Related Websites

The Dustbowl - A Learning Activity
    www.humanities-interactive.org/texas/dustbowl/
    dustbowl_teacher.htm
What is a Dust Bowl?
    www.infinet.com/~baugust/dust.html

Keep on Reading

Agnes May Gleason, Walsenburg, Colorado, 1933 by Kathleen Duey (Aladdin, 1998). Agnes struggles to help her father and family by working hard on the farm.

Nothing to Fear by Jackie French Koller (Harcourt Brace, 1993). Danny's strength and perseverance help his family survive the Depression.

Red-Dirt Jessie by Anna Myers (Puffin, 1997). Their Oklahoma farm hit hard by the Depression, Jessie's father gives up until Jessie takes charge.

Treasures in the Dust by Tracey Porter (HarperCollins, 1997). Two girls tell their family stories that take place during the Oklahoma Dust Bowl.

Goodbye, Walter Malinski by Helen Recorvits (Frances Foster Books, 1999). Caught in the midst of the Depression, poverty takes its toll on this immigrant family.

Song of the Trees by Mildred D. Taylor (Laurel-Leaf, 1996). Times are hard but Cassie Logan and her family fight to save the forest surrounding their house.

Lily's Crossing
Patricia Reilly Giff

Plot Summary

Every year Lily looks forward to summering at Rockaway Beach with her grandmother and father. In the summer of 1944 her father is sent to France and Lily is despondent until she befriends Albert, a Hungarian war orphan. Lily, an inveterate liar, sees "spies" everywhere and involves Albert in her imaginative and increasingly dangerous schemes.

Tips

This partially autobiographical novel marks a change from Giff's previous light-hearted series books. The award-winning audio version of this story is unabridged and is an excellent alternative to reading the entire book aloud. Hook potential readers by sharing the first three chapters or the Book Clip below.

Related Tips

www.randomhouse.com/teachers/guides/lily.html

Author Information

Patricia Reilly Giff loved to read as a child and wanted to be a writer early on. She was trained as a teacher and finally, after working with kids for a long time, Giff decided to pursue a writing career. Well known (and loved) for her humorous Polk Street Kids series, Giff felt compelled to write Lily's story.

Rockaway Beach during World War II was part of Giff's own childhood. She has vivid memories of the invasion of 1944 and the liberation of Paris. But most importantly, Giff recollects the power and importance of friendship and wants her readers to know that love does make a difference.

Related Author Resources

www.randomhouse.com/teachers/guides/giff.html

www.penguinputnam.com/catalog/yreader/authors/2048_biography.html

www.doubleday.com/teachersbdd/giff.html

Book Clip

Lily swallowed. She thought of her list of problems: *Number 1:* Lies, and then the second list, the list of solutions. Right up there on top was the promise not to tell a lie ever again, not even a tiny little one, much less one of those gigantic ones about her aunt being an important U.S. spy against the Nazis. (page 14, paperback edition)

Just the Facts

LC 96-23021. 180p. 1997. $15.95 (ISBN 0-385-32142-2). Delacorte Press.

Paperback. 1999. $4.99 (ISBN 0-440-41453-9). Yearling.

Audio book. Unabridged, 3 hrs., 30 min. $19.99 (ISBN 0-553-52529 8) Bantam Doubleday Dell Audio.

Genre: historical fiction

Themes: World War II, families, refugees, grandmothers, fathers, lies, fear, guilt, summer vacations, letters, separation, rescue, spies, friendship, swimming, piano playing, single parent families, radios, war orphans

Readability: Fifth grade

Interest Level: Fifth through eighth grade

Review Citations:

Booklist 93(11):941 Feb 1, 1997

Bulletin of the Center for Children's Books 50(9):282 Apr 1997

Horn Book Magazine 73(2):198 Mar/Apr 1997

Publishers Weekly 244(3):403 Jan 20, 1997

School Library Journal 43(2):103 Feb 1997

Everything about the war in Europe is scary and exciting, sending Lily's already active imagination into overdrive. This puts both Lily and her new friend Albert in danger's path as *Lily's Crossing* comes to pass.

Curriculum Connections

History (World War II, Spies, Spying)

Lily is fascinated by spies, suspects nearly everyone, and is aware of the government's "Loose Lips Sink Ships" policy with ten rules for safeguarding military information. The following will appeal to students with interests similar to Lily's: *Spy Book: The Encyclopedia of Espionage* by Norman Polmar (Random House, 1996); *Brassey's Book of Espionage* by John Laffin (Brasseys, 1997); *A Century of Spies: Intelligence in the Twentieth Century* by Jeffrey T. Richelson (Oxford University Press, 1995); *The Puzzle Palace: Inside the National Security Agency, America's Most Secret Intelligence Organization* by James Bamford (Penguin, 1983); *Spy* by Richard Platt (Eyewitness, 1996); *The Ultimate Spy Book* by H. Keith Melton (Dorling Kindersley, 1996); and *Espionage: The Greatest Spy Operations of the Twentieth Century* by Ernest Volkman (John Wiley, 1995).

Related Websites

Eye Witness: History Through the Eyes of Those Who Lived It — Loose Lips Sink Ships
www.ibiscom.com/lslips.htm

Central Intelligence Agency
www.cia.gov/cia/ciahome.html

History (Victory Gardens, Rations, Spam, Homefront, World War II)

Like most Americans, Lily and her grandmother had a fairly limited diet due to food shortages and rationing. Students will be interested in learning more about this time of sacrifice. Provide them with *Spam: A Biography* by Carolyn Wyman (Harvest Books, 1999); *V for Victory: America's Home Front During World War II* by Stan Cohen (Motorbooks International, 1991); *V Is for Victory: America Remembers World War II* by Kathleen Krull (Knopf, 1995); *Rosie the Riveter: Women Working on the Homefront in World War II* by Penny Colman (Crown, 1995); and *Doing Our Part: American Women on the Home Front During World War II* by Susan Sinnott (Franklin Watts, 1995).

Related Websites

Hooray for the Home Front
www.personal.psu.edu/users/l/e/lek105/

World War II: The Homefront
http://hyperion.advanced.org/15511/

At Home During World War II
www.pomperaug.com/socstud/stumuseum/web/ARHwww3.htm

World War II Posters Database
www.library.nwu.edu/govpub/collections/wwii-posters/

History (World War II, Refugees, War Orphans)

Lily's friend Albert was sent away from his Hungarian home to Canada and then the United States to keep him safe during the war. This was true for thousands of European children who were evacuated to Wales, the U.S., Australia, New Zealand, South Africa, and Canada. Students can research this topic further, including the tragic sinking of the ship *The City of Benares*, which brought an end to the evacuations. Provide books such as *Kindertransport* by Olga Levy Drucker (Henry Holt, 1995) and *Ten Thousand Children: True Stories Told by Children Who Escaped the Holocaust on the Kindertransport* with epilogues by Anne L. Fox and Eva Abraham-Podietz (Behrman House, 1998).

Related Websites

British Evacuees in America During World War II
http://xroads.virginia.edu/~JOURNAL/JAC/british.html

Keep on Reading

"Who Was That Masked Man, Anyway?" by Avi (Orchard, 1992). Toward the end of World War II, Frankie, an incorrigible snoop, plots to drive the family's boarder away and create a romance.

War Boy: A Country Childhood by Michael Foreman (Arcade, 1989). Foreman recalls his boyhood during World War II.

Stepping on Cracks by Mary Downing Hahn (Clarion, 1991). Two patriotic sixth-grade girls discover the school bully is hiding his pacifist brother during World War II.

The Sky Is Falling by Kit Pearson (Viking, 1989). Nora and her younger brother are evacuated to Canada from war torn England.

Under the Blood Red Sun by Graham Salisbury (Delacorte, 1994). The attack on Pearl Harbor changed the daily lives of Japanese American citizens like eighth-grader Tomi Nakajis.

Don't You Know There's a War On? by James Stevenson (Greenwillow, 1992). Watercolor sketches and the author's memories reveal glimpses of daily life in America between 1942–1945.

1998
HONOR

Ella Enchanted
Gail Carson Levine

Plot Summary

An unfortunate gift of absolute obedience was bestowed upon Ella at birth by a foolish fairy. The strong-willed Ella struggles with this curse but has help from her mother and fairy godmother. But when Ella's mother dies, her world changes dramatically. She has to deal not only with the curse, but also with her changed circumstances—finishing school, a wicked stepmother, conniving stepsisters, and her father's financial losses. A quest to find the fairy and reverse the curse is unsuccessful.

Tips

The 1998 Cinderella movie *Ever After* (1998) can be used as an introduction or culminating event. To entice potential readers, suggest they read the first chapter online from the publisher's website below.

Related Tips

www.harperchildrens.com/features/chapone.htm
www.slc.k12.ut.us/clau/clau9ee.htm

Author Information

Although she never intended to become a writer, Gail Carson Levine was a member of the Scribble Scrabble Club in elementary school and some of her poetry was published in a high school poetry anthology. Levine grew up in New York and planned to be a painter. However, when she took a writing and illustrating class, she discovered she was much more interested in writing. Levine lives in New York with her husband in a two hundred-year old farmhouse.

Ella Enchanted began as a class project and turned into a novel. Levine had always thought Cinderella was a goody-two-shoes and she wanted to portray her with a sense of rebellion.

Book Clip

A curse of obedience was bestowed upon Ella at birth—with terrible results.

> Anyone could control me with an order. It had to be a direct command… A wish or a request had no effect… If someone told me to hop on one

Just the Facts

LC 96-30734. 240p. 1997. $14.95 (ISBN 0-06-027510-3). HarperCollins.

Paperback. 1998. $4.95 (ISBN 0-06-440705-5). HarperTrophy.

Audio book. Unabridged, 5 hours. 1998. $21.95 (ISBN 0-553-52528-X). Bantam Doubleday Dell Audio.

Genres: fantasy, humor

Themes: Cinderella, spells, fate, obedience, magic, friendship, love, courage, letters, princes, mythical creatures, heroines, death, education, godmothers, step-families, trading, gifts, royalty, zoos, greed, manners, romance

Readability: Fifth grade

Interest Level: Fifth through ninth grade

Review Citations:

Booklist 93(16):1423 Apr 15, 1997

Bulletin of the Center for Children's Books 50(9):327 May 1997

English Journal 88(3):124 Jan 1999

Horn Book Magazine 63(3):325 May/June 1997

Publishers Weekly 244(13):75 Mar 31, 1997

School Library Journal 43(4):138 Apr 1997

foot for a day and a half, I'd have to do it. And hopping on one foot wasn't the worst order I could be given. If you commanded me to cut off my own head, I'd have to do it. (page 4-5, paperback edition)

Ella may be enchanted but she certainly isn't safe. Keeping the curse a secret and searching for a way to undo it becomes her quest.

Curriculum Connections

Art (Mythical Creatures)

Many mythical creatures dwell in Ella's world. Some of them are gnomes, ogres, unicorns, and fairies. Students can create original drawings of these characters based on Levine's descriptions, and develop a gallery of exotic creatures. For more complete descriptions provide Eric Carle's *Dragons and Other Creatures That Never Were* by Laura Whipple (Putnam, 1991); *Treasury of Fantastic and Mythological Creatures: 1087 Renderings from Historic Sources* by Richard Huber (Dover, 1981); *The Magic of Mythical Creatures* by Colleayn O. Mastin (Grasshopper Books, 1997); or send students to the 398.2 section of your school or public library.

Related Websites

Mythical Creatures: Greek Mythology
   www.geocities.com/Athens/Oracle/5545/creatures.html

Gareth Long's Encyclopedia of Monsters, Mythical Creatures and Fabulous Beasts
   http://webhome.idirect.com/~donlong/monsters/Html/awards.htm

Writing (Creative Writing, Behavior, Values, Curses)

Generally obedience is considered to be a good characteristic, but that is definitely not the case for Ella. Students can select other positive behaviors or values (such as honesty, bravery, or cleanliness) and write a story where such characteristics would be counterproductive or worse!

Writing (Reference Books, Fairies)

In groups or individually, write and illustrate a "Fairy Rules and Properties" reference book from the information readers learn about fairies from *Ella Enchanted* ("we can't stop dying," page 23; "We are too tall for our feet," page 26; etc.) and other books featuring fairies. Helpful books include *Diane Goode's Book of Giants and Little People* by Diane Goode (Dutton, 1997); *Fairies* by Elizabeth Ratisseau (Blue Lantern Studio, 1999); *The Light Princess* by George MacDonald (Sunburst, 1992); *Encyclopedia of Fairies* by Katharine Briggs (Random House, 1978); and *Faeries* edited by David Larkin (Abrams, 1995).

Related Websites

Hidden Ireland: A Guide to Irish Fairies
   www.irelandseye.com/animation/intro.html

Keep on Reading

The Forest Family by Joan Bodger (Tundra, 1999). Sisters Rosy and Daisy survive in the forest with their talented mother in this recasting of the Brothers Grimm's "Snow White and Rose Red."

Just Ella by Margaret Peterson Haddix (Simon & Schuster, 1999). Ella refuses to marry the empty-headed Prince Charming and is sent to the dungeon.

Cinderella 2000 by Mavis Jukes (Delacorte, 1999). Fourteen-year-old Ashley Ella is invited to a New Millennium's Eve party but her scheming stepmother and stepsisters may ruin her plans.

Beauty: A Retelling of the Story of Beauty and the Beast by Robin McKinley (HarperCollins, 1985). Proud of her own intelligence, Beauty is able to help her sisters when they become poverty-stricken.

Spinners by Donna Jo Napoli and Richard Tchen. (Dutton, 1999). The mysterious spinner Rumplestiltskin rescues young Saskia, who spins wonderful yarns and believes she is the miller's daughter.

The Magic Circle by Donna Jo Napoli (Puffin, 1995). Here is a retelling of the Hansel and Gretel story from the misunderstood witch's point of view.

1998
HONOR

Wringer
Jerry Spinelli

Plot Summary

Nine-year-old Palmer dreads his tenth birthday because then he'll have to become a wringer—the boys who break the necks of pigeons who are injured but not killed during the town's annual fundraising pigeon shoot. His worry is compounded when he secretly befriends a pigeon that becomes his pet and companion throughout the school year. Palmer struggles with peer pressure, friendships, and being true to himself.

Tips

The forty chapters are placed between two facsimiles of news articles reflecting the real events that inspired Spinelli to write this book. Read aloud the first three chapters to hook potential readers. Students can read the first chapter of this book online from the publisher's website, below.

Related Tips

www.harperchildrens.com/features/chapone.htm

Author Information

Jerry Spinelli was born in Norristown, Pennsylvania. He and his wife, Eileen (also a writer) have six children. One of his first writing experiences was writing a poem after his high school football team won a big game. It was published in the local newspaper and Spinelli has been writing ever since. As a kid, Spinelli played in five different sports and wanted to be a professional shortstop.

Wringer was inspired by news articles about a small town near Spinelli's home where pigeons are shot annually as a fundraiser. He wondered about the boys who had to clear away the dead birds and finish off the wounded ones.

Related Author Resources

Knots in My Yo-Yo String: The Autobiography of a Kid by Jerry Spinelli (Knopf, 1998)

Jerry Spinelli by Kimberley Clark (Learning Works, 1999)

Video: *Good Conversation! A Talk with Jerry Spinelli.* Color, 20 min. (Tim Podell Productions, 1994).

www.carr.lib.md.us/authco/spinelli-j.htm

http://edupaperback.org/authorbios/spinell.html

Book Clip

Palmer hated the park. He never played there, never swung on the swings, never slid down the

Just the Facts

LC 96-37897. 192p. 1997. $15.89 (ISBN 0-06-024913-7). HarperCollins.

Paperback. $5.95 (ISBN 0-06-440578-8). HarperTrophy.

Audio book. Unabridged, 4.75 hours. 1997. $34 (ISBN 0-7887-1798-7). Recorded Books.

Genre: contemporary realistic fiction

Themes: pigeons, coming-of-age, rituals, friendship, courage, violence, guns, fathers and sons, mothers and sons, bullies, teasing, secrets, heroes, belonging, fund-raising, trophies

Readability: Fourth grade
Interest Level: Fourth through eighth grade
Review Citations:

Booklist 94(1):118 Sept 1, 1997

Bulletin of the Center for Children's Books 51(8):67 Oct 1997

Horn Book Magazine 73(5):581 Sept/Oct 1997

Publishers Weekly 244(22):72 June 2, 1997

School Library Journal 43(9):226 Sept 1997

sliding board, never fed the ducks, never watched a softball game. Most especially, he never went near the soccer field. For in one month, four short weeks after his birthday, the soccer field would become, as it did every year, a place of horror. (page 15, hardback and paperback editions)

Why is Palmer so afraid of the soccer field? What horrible thing happens there every year, four weeks after his birthday? Readers of *Wringer* will know.

Curriculum Connections

Science (Literature, Birds, Pigeons)

Raising homing pigeons has been a popular hobby for decades. Invite an expert to speak to students about this hobby and/or provide some of the following information for further research: *Aloft: A Meditation on Pigeons and Pigeon-Flying* by Stephen Bodio (Lyons & Burford, 1990); *Pigeons* by Dorothy Hinshaw Patent (Clarion, 1997); and *Pigeons and Doves* by Ray Nofsinger and Jim Hargrove (Children's Press, 1992).

Stories with pigeons include Jane Kurtz's Ethiopian tale about homing pigeons *Only a Pigeon* (Simon & Schuster, 1997); David Macaulay's wordless *Rome Antics* (Houghton Mifflin, 1997); and Jeannie Baker's *Home in the Sky* (Greenwillow, 1984).

Related Websites

The Pigeon Cote
http://members.aol.com/duiven/cote.htm

The American Racing Pigeon Union
www.pigeon.org/

National Pigeon Association
http://npausa.com/

Social Issues (Guns, Children and Guns, Current Events, Gun Control, Politics, Gun Safety)

Even though Palmer and his friends aren't actually shooting pigeons, the issue of guns, children, and violence can be addressed in relation to this book. Create a classroom library with stories that focus on guns to spark discussion on related topics—gun control, national registry, hunter safety, hunter age policies, and the place of the National Rifle Association in politics. Include some or all of the following books: Gary Paulsen's *The Rifle* (Harcourt, 1995); *Twelve Shots: Outstanding Short Stories about Guns* edited by Harry Mazer (Delacorte, 1997); *Making Up Megaboy* by Virginia Walter (DK, 1998); *The One-Eyed Cat* by Paula Fox (Macmillan, 1984); *Home Wars* by Dorothy R. Miller (Simon & Schuster, 1997); and the picture book *Just One*

Flick of a Finger written by Marybeth Lorbiecki and illustrated by David Diaz (Dial, 1996).

Related Websites

Children's Defense Fund: Children and Guns
www.childrensdefense.org/youthviolence/
childandguns. html

Sociology (Bullies, Self-esteem,)

Palmer is thrilled to finally be part of a gang even though it involves a feared initiation rite and tormenting a girl who had been his best friend. Most children deal with teasing and bullies at one time or another. Use the following materials to provoke a class discussion on this important issue: *How to Handle Bullies, Teasers and Other Meanies: A Book That Takes the Nuisance Out of Name Calling and Other Nonsense* by Kate Cohen-Posey (Rainbow, 1995); *Bullies Are a Pain in the Brain* by Trevor Romain (Free Spirit, 1997); and *Bullying* by Pete Sanders (Millbrook, 1996).

Related Websites

Bully-Proof Your School
www.education-world.com/a_admin/admin018.shtml

Dealing with Bullies
www.safechild.org/bullies.htm

Keep on Reading

Fight for Honor by Carin Greenberg Baker (Penguin/Puffin, 1992). Lee wonders whether he can use his self-defense skills to take on the school bully.

Lostman's River by Cynthia DeFelice (Macmillan, 1994). Thirteen-year-old Tyler observes poachers killing beautiful birds and must make up his mind about his own values.

The One-Eyed Cat by Paula Fox (Simon & Schuster, 1984). Despite explicit orders not to, Ned takes out the forbidden gun and later is haunted by the knowledge that he may have injured a cat.

Batty Hattie by Virginia Nielsen (Marshall Cavendish, 1999). Harriet takes care of an abandoned bat and helps her classmates appreciate these misunderstood animals.

The Pennywhistle Tree by Doris Buchanan Smith (Putnam, 1991). When a bully moves next door, life is disrupted for Jonathan and his friends and family.

The Bully of Barkham Street by Mary Stoltz (HarperCollins, 1985). Two boys explore good and evil as they journey toward adolescence.

1999
MEDAL
Holes
Louis Sachar

Plot Summary

After Stanley Yelnats is wrongfully accused of stealing, he can choose jail or a juvenile detention camp called Camp Green Lake. He'd never been to camp but Camp Green Lake is nobody's idea of fun. Every day Stanley and his fellow inmates must dig a five by five by five foot hole in the dried up lake bed. Stanley befriends an illiterate boy, saves him from injustice, finds the buried treasure, and breaks his family's curse.

Tips

Three storylines eventually intersect in this three-part, fifty-chapter book. While this could be confusing, most readers will catch on quickly. Read it aloud to entertain an entire class, or provide the unabridged audio version. To hook independent readers, read aloud the first chapter.

Related Tips

www.plainfield.k12.in.us/hschool/webq/webq91/index.htm

Author Information

Born in New York and educated in California, Louis Sachar prefers writing children's books to being an attorney, tries not to write down to kids, and writes what he thinks is funny. When Sachar was in college he took a job as a teacher's aide for $2.04 a day. His job was to be the "Noon Time Supervisor" where he played games with the kids and was called "Louis, the Yard Teacher."

Related Author Resources

http://edupaperback.org/authorbios/Sacharl.html

www.pbs.org/newshour/bb/entertainment/july-dec98/sacher_11 25.html

Newbery Acceptance Speech: *Horn Book Magazine* 75(5):410 July/Aug 1999

Book Clip

After Stanley is sent to a juvenile detention camp called Camp Green Lake, he finds out his punishment is to dig a five by five by five foot hole every day in the dried up lake bed.

> One thing was certain: They weren't just digging to "build character." They were definitely looking for something. And whatever they were looking for, they were looking in the wrong place. Stanley

Just the Facts

LC 97-45011. 233p. 1998. $16 (ISBN 0-374-332265-7). Farrar, Straus & Giroux.

Audio book. Unabridged, 4.5 hours. 1999. $23.98 (ISBN 0-807-28071-2). Listening Library.

Genres: contemporary realistic fiction, humor, mystery

Themes: friendship, truth, justice, fate, survival, buried treasure, tall tales, juvenile detention, stealing, camp, nicknames, deserts, guilt, curses, inventions, innocence, goals, literacy, greed, racism, character, redemption, bullies

Readability: Sixth grade

Interest Level: Sixth through ninth grade

Review Citations:

Booklist 95(14):1302 Mar 15, 1999

Bulletin of the Center for Children's Books 52(1):29 Sept 1998

Horn Book Magazine 75(3):358 May 1999

Publishers Weekly 246:28(20 July 12, 1999

School Library Journal 45(9):165 Sept 1999

gazed out across the lake, toward the spot where he had been digging yesterday when he found the gold tube. He dug the hole into his memory. (page 71, hardback edition)

Getting back to that particular hole—and finding the treasure is only part of the "hole" story.

Curriculum Connections

History (Archeology)

Although Stanley and cohorts find their constant digging less than desirable, digging holes and discovering things is commonplace for archeologists. Students can find out more about what archeologists do by examining books like *Dig This! How Archaeologists Uncover Our Past* by Michael Avi-Yonah (Lerner, 1993); *Archaeologists Dig for Clues* by Kate Duke (HarperCollins, 1997); *The Children's Atlas of Lost Treasures* by Struan Reid (Millbrook, 1997); *The Iceman* by Don Lessem (Crown, 1994); *Tutankhamun: The Life and Death of a Pharaoh* by David Murdoch (DK Publishing, 1998); and *Breaking Ground, Breaking Silence: The Story of New York's African Burial Ground* by Joyce Hansen (Henry Holt, 1998).

Related Websites

Archeology: Newton's Apple
   http://ericir.syr.edu/Projects/Newton/11/archeogy.html

Archaeological Adventure in Greece
   www.richmond.edu/~ed344/webquests/archaeology/webquest4.html

Center for Indigenous Research – Virtual Village
   http://virtualelpaso.com/archaeology/vv/index.htm

Language (Palindromes, Word Play, Writing)

Stanley Yelnats is a palindrome—a word or sentence that reads the same forward and backward. Writing palindromes is creative and fun, and students will love the word play. Provide samples for students from books such as Jon Agee's *So Many Dynamos!* (Farrar, Straus & Giroux, 1994); *Go Hang a Salami! I'm a Lasagna Hog! And Other Palindromes* (Farrar, Straus & Giroux, 1992); and *Sit on a Potato Pan, Otis! More Palindromes* (Farrar, Straus & Giroux, 1999); plus *Autumn: An Alphabet Acrostic* by Steven Schnur (Clarion, 1997); and *Too Hot to Hoot: Funny Palindrome Riddles* by Marvin Terban (Houghton Mifflin, 1985).

Related Websites

WordPlay
   http://fun-with-words.com/
Palindromes Galore!
   www.jps.net/msyu/palindromes/

Legends (Writing, Interviews)

Stanley's family stories are legendary, and many families and towns have similar larger-than-life stories from their pasts. Send students out into the community to discover local legends. Compile, publish, and share—with your library, historical museum, and newspaper. Create a website of the finished product.

Related Websites

The Family History Project
   www.kidlink.org/KIDPROJ/FamHistory/data.html
Oral History questions- The Gene Pool
   www.rootsweb.com/~genepool/oralhist.htm
Using Oral History: Conducting the Interview
   www.cms.ccsd.k12.co.us/ss/SONY/orbeta1/conduct.htm

Keep on Reading

Lord of the Flies by William Golding (Perigee, 1959). English schoolboys, stranded on a deserted island, invent their own society.

Slot Machine by Chris Lynch (HarperCollins, 1995). Fourteen-year-old Elvin is overweight and off to a camp where (at first) he doesn't fit in.

The Blood and Thunder Adventure on Hurricane Peak by Margaret Mahy (Macmillan, 1989). Inventors, writers of blood and thunder stories, and magicians conspire for a hilarious adventure.

Clockwork by Philip Pullman (Arthur K. Levine, 1998). Two stories intersect with a clockwork figure and a knight.

The Westing Game by Ellen Raskin (Dutton, 1989). Sixteen heirs gather for the reading of an unusual will.

Maniac Magee by Jerry Spinelli (Little, Brown, 1990). The legendary Maniac Magee has no home but touches the lives of all who know him—black and white, young and old.

1999

HONOR

A Long Way From Chicago
Richard Peck

Plot Summary

From 1929 to 1935 Joey and his younger sister Mary Alice make annual summer trips from Chicago to visit their grandmother in her rural town. The grandmother creates outlandish schemes to get even with bullies and villains, to teach a lesson, or to improve someone else's life. Her brand of justice skirts the law and surprises her grandchildren, who are mostly reluctant (but highly entertained) participants.

Tips

A prologue and final chapter (set in 1942) frame the seven episodic chapters which each feature a summer visit. Any of the seven chapters can stand alone as a short story. The terrific language, humorous and outrageous occurrences, and short chapter lengths make them perfect for reading aloud. Richard Peck is a reading aloud advocate and has written a marvelous poem entitled "Twenty Minutes a Day." It is available on the Penguin/Putnam website listed in Related Author Resources.

Author Information

A prolific and award-winning author of books for young adults and children, Richard Peck writes about contemporary issues as well as humor, mystery, and historical novels. He grew up in the Midwest and, like his father, had a passion for cars and Mark Twain. An only child, surrounded by adults, Peck regularly listened to family stories about the old days. He planned to be a teacher and majored in English in college. After serving in the army for two years, Peck attended graduate school and then began a ten-year teaching and editing stint. In 1971 he started writing fulltime.

Related Author Resources

Anonymously Yours by Richard Peck (Beech Tree, 1995)

www.randomhouse.com/teachersbdd/peck.html

www.carr.lib.md.us/mae/peck.htm

www.penguinputnam.com/catalog/yreader/authors/2237_biography.html

Book Clip

Just to spite the smug citizens, Grandma insists on holding a wake and a proper burial for Shotgun

Just the Facts

LC 98-10953. 148p. 1998. $15.99 (ISBN 0-8037-2290-7). Dial Books for Young Readers.

Audio book. Unabridged. 1999. $23.98 (ISBN 0-8072-8125-5). Listening Library.

Genres: historical fiction, humor

Themes: grandmothers, brothers and sisters, Great Depression, small town life, justice, generosity, cooking, county fairs, memories, Prohibition, pranks, ghost stories, charity, summer vacations, truth, contests

Readability: Sixth grade

Interest Level: Fourth through eighth grade

Review Citations:

Booklist 95(1):113 Sept 1, 1998

Bulletin of the Center for Children's Books 52(2):69 Oct 1998

Horn Book Magazine 74(6):738 Nov 1998

Publishers Weekly 245(27):61 July 6, 1998

School Library Journal 44(10:144 Oct 1998

Cheatum, the town vagrant. His coffin is on display in her parlor, watched carefully by Grandma and her two grandchildren, Joe and Mary Alice. Joey has been sitting somewhat obediently when to his horror he notices …

> … the gauze that hung down over the open coffin moved. Twitched … it wrinkled into a wad as if somebody had snagged it. As if a feeble hand had reached up from the coffin depths in one last desperate attempt to live before the dirt was shoveled in. Every hair on my head stood up. (page 14, hardback edition)

This is just one summer adventure for Joey and Mary Alice with their Grandmother—who lives a long way from Chicago.

Curriculum Connections

History (Timelines, 1930s)

Peck presents a vivid look at life for many Americans during the 1930s. For a better understanding of the political, social, and economic climate in the United States and the development of the arts during this time, students can develop timelines with explanations of various events for each of the years. Useful materials include *Growing Up in the Great Depression* by Richard Wormser (Atheneum, 1994); *The Great Depression in American History* by David K. Fremon (Enslow, 1997); *Children's History of the 20th Century* (DK Publishing, 1999); *The Century for Young People* by Peter Jennings, Todd Brewster, and Jennifer Armstrong (Doubleday, 1999); and *Oxford Children's Book of the 20th Century: A Concise Guide to a Century of Contrast and Change* by Stewart Ross (Oxford University Press, 1999).

Related Websites

America in the 1930s
    http://xroads.virginia.edu/~1930s/home_1.html

The Media History Project: 20th Century: Fourth Decade
    www.mediahistory.com/time/1930s.html

The 1930s in Print - Stories that made the News!
    http://xroads.virginia.edu/g/1930s/PRINT/timeline.html

History (1920, Prohibition, Bootlegging, Gangsters, Speakeasies, Current Events)

Even though drinking and making alcohol was illegal because of Prohibition, Grandma and others (even the sheriff) regularly made and drank their own brews. A rise in crime followed the Prohibition law in 1920. Making and distributing illegal liquor became a giant industry and rival gangs fought for control of bootleg liquor and speakeasies and the resulting profits. Students can learn more about this period of American history, including the reasons the Prohibition law was repealed. Invite contrast and comparison to current laws on controlled substances. Provide supplementary materials such as *Farewell, John Barleycorn: Prohibition in the United States* by Martin Hintz (Lerner, 1996) and *Prohibition: America Makes Alcohol Illegal* by Daniel Cohen (Millbrook, 1995).

In addition, the gangster element will interest many students. Capitalizing on the Hollywood version of gangsters that most students have, begin a study of the real history of gangsters (Al "Scarface" Capone, George "Bugs" Moran, Bonnie and Clyde, etc.) and their activities, Prohibition, and the economic and social life of speakeasies and bootlegging. Extend this activity to current events, focusing on the anti smoking movement, gang activity, and current tobacco laws and financial settlements. Materials of interest include *Al Capone and the Roaring Twenties* by David C. King (Blackbirch, 1998) and *The Roaring Twenties* by Richard Conrad Stein (Children's Press, 1994).

Related Websites

The Roaring Twenties: An Integrated Lesson
    www2.educ.ksu.edu/faculty/ParmleyJ/Block%20One%20S97/TeamNine.html

Temperance and Prohibition
    www.cohums.ohio-state.edu/history/projects/prohibition/

Compton's Encyclopedia: Prohibition
    www.optonline.com/comptons/ceo/03867_A.html

The Mob in the 20's
    www.umi.com/hp/Support/K12/GreatEvents/Mob.html

Prohibition in the 1920s: Thirteen Years That Damaged America: A term paper
    www.geocities.com/Athens/Troy/4399/

Literature (Grandmothers, Picture Books for Older Readers)

Joey's grandmother is a unique character and she has a special relationship with Joey and his sister. Frequently children develop remarkable kinships with grandparents that transcend age differences. Celebrate grandmothers by hosting a festive event and inviting grandmothers (real and adopted). Assemble a classroom collection of books featuring diverse grandmothers. Include picture books like *Busy Day for a Good Grandmother* by Margaret Mahy (Margaret McElderry, 1993) and *Our Granny* by Margaret Wild (Ticknor & Fields, 1994); as well as novels such as *Toning the Sweep* by Angela Johnson (Orchard, 1993) and *Granny the Pag* by Nina Bawden (Clarion, 1996).

Keep on Reading

Granny the Pag by Nina Bawden (Clarion, 1996). Neglected by her famous actor parents, Catriona is raised by her eccentric grandmother and develops special feelings toward her.

Ida Early Comes over the Mountain by Robert Burch (Puffin, 1990). During the Depression years, the hilarious Ida Early comes to take care of Mr. Sutton's motherless children.

Bud, Not Buddy by Christopher Paul Curtis (Delacorte, 1999). Ten-year-old Buddy runs away from the orphanage to look for his father and finds adventure and kindness during the Depression.

The Great Brain by John Fitzgerald (Yearling, 1972). Tom Fitzgerald's exploits and schemes are outrageous and funny.

Harris and Me by Gary Paulsen (Harcourt Brace, 1993). Growing up in a town hadn't prepared the eleven-year-old narrator for a new world of adventure on his cousins' farm.

When Zachary Beaver Came to Town by Kimberly Willis Holt (Henry Holt, 1999). Toby Wilson's saddest summer also turns out to be his most interesting when the fattest boy in the world arrives in Toby's town.

Appendix A

Resources

Carpenter, Humphrey, and Mari Prichard. *The Oxford Companion to Children's Literature* (Oxford University Press, 1984).

Gillespie, John T., and Corinne J. Naden. *The Newbery Companion: Booktalk and Related Materials for Newbery Medal and Honor Books* (Libraries Unlimited, 1996).

Jones, Dolores Blythe. *Children's Literature Awards and Winners: A Directory of Prizes, Authors, and Illustrators* (Neal-Schuman, 1983).

Kingman, Lee, ed. *Newbery and Caldecott Medal Books 1966–1975* (Horn Book, 1975).

———. *Newbery and Caldecott Medal Books 1976–1985* (Horn Book, 1986).

Licciardo-Musso, Lori. *Teaching with Favorite Newbery Books* (Scholastic Professional, 1999).

The Newbery and Caldecott Awards: A Guide to the Medal and Honor Books 1999 (American Library Association, 1999).

Paterson, Linda Kauffman, and Marilyn Leathers Solt. *Newbery and Caldecott Medal and Honor Books: An Annotated Bibliography.* (G.K. Hall, 1982).

Story-Huffman, Ru. *Newbery on the Net: Reading & Internet Activities* (Alleyside, 1998).

Townsend, John Rowe, ed. *John Newbery and His Books: Trade and Plumb-Cake For Ever, Huzza!* (Scarecrow, 1994).

Welsh, Charles. *A Bookseller of the Last Century (Being Some Account of the Life of John Newbery and of the Books He Published with a Notice of the Later Newberys).* (Augustus M. Kelley, 1885, 1972).

Journal of Youth Services (Joys) is published quarterly by the American Association of School Librarians (AASL) and is the official source for information about the Newbery and Caldecott Awards.

For official Newbery information:

Newbery Medal Home Page
www.ala.org/alsc/newbery.html

Complete Listing of Newbery Medal and Honor Books, 1922–2000

1922 *The Story of Mankind.* Hendrik Willem Van Loon (Liveright)

Honors

The Old Tobacco Shop. William Bowen (Macmillan)

The Golden Fleece and the Heroes Who Lived before Achilles. Padraic Colum (Macmillan)

The Great Quest. Charles Hawes (Little)

Cedric the Forester. Bernard Marshall (Appleton)

Windy Hill. Cornelia Meigs (Macmillan)

1923 *The Voyages of Doctor Dolittle.* Hugh Lofting (Lippincott)

Honor: No Record

1924 *The Dark Frigate.* Charles Hawes (Little)

Honor: No Record

1925 *Tales from Silver Lands.* Charles Finger (Doubleday)

Honors

Nicholas. Anne Carroll Moore (Putnam)

Dream Coach. Anne Parrish (Macmillan)

1926 *Shen of the Sea.* Arthur Bowie Crisman (Dutton)

Honor

Voyagers. Padraic Colum (Macmillan)

1927 *Smoky, the Cowhorse.* Will James (Scribner)

Honor: No Record

1928 *Gay Neck, the Story of a Pigeon.* Dhan Gopal Mukerji (Dutton)

Honors

Downright Dencey. Caroline Snedeker (Doubleday)

The Wonder Smith and His Son. Ella Young (Longmans)

1929 *The Trumpeter of Krakow.* Eric P. Kelly (Macmillan)

Honors

Pigtail of Ah Lee Ben Loo. John Bennett (Longmans)

Millions of Cats. Wanda Gag (Coward)

The Boy Who Was. Grace Hallock (Dutton)

Clearing Weather. Cornelia Meigs (Little)

Runaway Papoose. Grace Moon (Doubleday)

Tod of the Fens. Elinor Whitney (Macmillan)

1930 *Hitty, Her First Hundred Years.* Rachel Field (Macmillan)

Honors

Vaino. Julia Davis Adams (Dutton)

Daughter of the Seine. Jeanette Eaton (Harper)

Jumping-Off Place. Marian Hurd Mcneely (Longmans)

Pran of Albania. Elizabeth Miller (Doubleday)

Little Blacknose. Hildegarde Swift (Harcourt)

Tangle-Coated Horse and Other Tales. Ella Young (Longmans)

1931 *The Cat Who Went to Heaven.* Elizabeth Coatsworth (Macmillan)

Honors

Mountains Are Free. Julia Davis Adams (Dutton)

Garram the Hunter. Herbert Best (Doubleday)

Meggy Macintosh. Elizabeth Janet Gray (Doubleday)

Spice and the Devil's Cave. Agnes Hewes (Knopf)

Queer Person. Ralph Hubbard (Doubleday)

Ood-Le-Uk the Wanderer. Alice Lide And Margaret Johansen (Little)

The Dark Star of Itza. Alida Malkus (Harcourt)

Floating Island. Anne Parrish (Harper)

1932 *Waterless Mountain.* Laura Adams Armer (Longmans)

Honors

Jane's Island. Marjorie Allee (Houghton)

Truce of the Wolf and Other Tales of Old Italy. Mary Gould Davis (Harcourt)

Calico Bush. Rachel Field (Macmillan)

The Fairy Circus. Dorothy Lathrop (Macmillan)

Out of the Flame. Eloise Lownsbery (Longmans)

Boy of the South Seas. Eunice Tietjens (Coward-Mccann)

1933 *Young Fu of the Upper Yangtze.* Elizabeth Lewis (Winston)

Honors

Children of the Soil. Nora Burglon (Doubleday)

Swift Rivers. Cornelia Meigs (Little)

The Railroad to Freedom. Hildegarde Swift (Harcourt)

1934 *Invincible Louisa.* Cornelia Meigs (Little)

Honors

Winged Girl of Knossos. Eric Berry, Pseud. for Allena Best (Appleton)
Big Tree of Bunlahy. Padraic Colum (Macmillan)
ABC Bunny. Wanda Gag (Coward)
Glory of the Seas. Agnes Hewes (Knopf)
Apprentice of Florence. Anne Kyle (Houghton)
New Land. Sarah Schmidt (Mcbride)
Swords of Steel. Elsie Singmaster (Houghton)
The Forgotten Daughter. Caroline Snedeker (Doubleday)

1935 *Dobry.* Monica Shannon (Viking)

Honors

Davy Crockett. Constance Rourke (Harcourt)
Pageant of Chinese History. Elizabeth Seeger (Longmans)
Day on Skates. Hilda Van Stockum (Harper)

1936 *Caddie Woodlawn.* Carol Ryrie Brink (Macmillan)

Honors

Young Walter Scott. Elizabeth Janet Gray (Viking)
The Good Master. Kate Seredy (Viking)
All Sail Set. Armstrong Sperry (Winston)
Hone, the Moose. Phil Strong (Dodd)

1937 *Roller Skates.* Ruth Sawyer (Viking)

Honors

Golden Basket. Ludwig Bemelmans (Viking)
Winterbound. Margery Bianco (Viking)
The Codfish Market. Agnes Hewes (Doubleday)
Whistler's Van. Idwal Jones (Viking)
Phoebe Fairchild: Her Book. Lois Lenski (Stokes)
Audubon. Constance Rourke (Harcourt)

1938 *The White Stag.* Kate Seredy (Viking)

Honors

Pecos Bill. James Cloyd Bowman (Little, Brown)
Bright Island. Mabel Robinson (Random)
On the Banks of Plum Creek. Laura Ingalls Wilder (Harper)

1939 *Thimble Summer.* Elizabeth Enright (Farrar and Rinehart)

Honors

Nino. Valenti Angelo (Viking)
Mr. Popper's Penguins. Richard and Florence Atwater (Little, Brown)
"Hello the Boat!" Phyllis Crawford (Holt)
Leader by Destiny: George Washington, Man and Patriot. Jeanette Eaton (Harcourt)
Penn. Elizabeth Janet Gray (Viking)

1940 *Daniel Boone.* James Daugherty (Viking)

Honors

Boy with a Pack. Stephen W. Meader (Harcourt)
Runner of the Mountain Tops. Mabel Robinson (Random House)
The Singing Tree. Kate Seredy (Viking)

By the Shores of Silver Lake. Laura Ingalls Wilder (Harper)

1941 *Call It Courage.* Armstrong Sperry (Macmillan)

Honors

Young Mac of Fort Vancouver. Mary Jane Carr (Crowell)
Blue Willow. Doris Gates (Viking)
Nansen. Anna Gertrude Hall (Viking)
The Long Winter. Laura Ingalls Wilder (Harper)

1942 *The Matchlock Gun.* Walter Edmonds (Dodd)

Honors

George Washington's World. Genevieve Foster (Scribner)
Down Ryton Water. Eva Roe Gaggin (Viking)
Indian Captive: The Story of Mary Jemison. Louis Lenski (Lippincott)
Little Town on the Prairie. Laura Ingalls Wilder (Harper)

1943 *Adam of the Road.* Elizabeth Jane Gray (Viking)

Honors

The Middle Moffat. Eleanor Estes (Harcourt)
"Have You Seen Tom Thumb?" Mabel Leigh Hunt (Lippincott)

1944 *Johnny Tremain.* Esther Forbes (Houghton)

Honors

Rufus M. Eleanor Estes (Harcourt)
Fog Magic. Julia Sauer (Viking)
These Happy Golden Years. Laura Ingalls Wilder (Harper)
Mountain Born. Elizabeth Yates (Coward)

1945 *Rabbit Hill.* Robert Lawson (Viking)

Honors

The Silver Pencil. Alice Dalgliesh (Scribner)
Lone Journey: The Life of Roger Williams. Jeanette Eaton (Harcourt)
The Hundred Dresses. Eleanor Estes (Harcourt)
Abraham Lincoln's World. Genevieve Foster (Scribner)

1946 *Strawberry Girl.* Lois Lenski (Lippincott)

Honors

Justin Morgan Had a Horse. Marguerite Henry (Rand McNally)
The Moved-Outsiders. Florence Crannell Means (Houghton)
New Found World. Katherine Shippen (Viking)
Bhimsa, the Dancing Bear. Christine Weston (Scribner)

1947 *Miss Hickory.* Carolyn Sherwin Bailey (Viking)

Honors

Wonderful Year. Nancy Barnes (Messner)
Big Tree. Mary and Conrad Buff (Viking)
The Avion My Uncle Flew. Cyrus Fisher, Pseud. for Darwin L. Teilhet (Appleton)
The Heavenly Tenants. William Maxwell (Harper)
The Hidden Treasure of Glaston. Eleanore Jewett (Viking)

1948 *The Twenty-One Balloons.* William Pene Du Bois (Viking)

Honors

The Quaint and Curious Quest of Johnny Longfoot. Catherine Besterman (Bobbs Merrill)
Pancakes—Paris. Claire Huchet Bishop (Viking)
The Cow-Tail Switch, and Other West African Stories. Harold Courlander (Holt)
Li Lun, Lad of Courage. Carolyn Treffinger (Abingdon)
Misty of Chincoteague. Marguerite Henry (Rand Mcnally)

1949 *King of the Wind.* Marguerite Henry (Rand Mcnally)

Honors

Story of the Negro. Arna Bontemps (Knopf)
Father's Dragon. Ruth Gannett (Random House)
Seabird. Holling C. Holling (Houghton)
Daughter of the Mountain. Louise Rankin (Viking)

1950 *The Door in the Wall.* Marguerite De Angeli (Doubleday)

Honors

Tree of Freedom. Rebecca Caudill (Viking)
The Blue Cat of Castle Town. Catherine Coblentz (Longmans)
George Washington. Genevieve Foster (Scribner)
Song of the Pines. Walter and Marion Havighurst (Winston)
Kildee House. Rutherford Montgomery (Doubleday)

1951 *Amos Fortune, Free Man.* Elizabeth Yates (Dutton)

Honors

Gandhi, Fighter Without a Sword. Jeanette Eaton (Morrow)
Better Known As Johnny Appleseed. Mabel Leigh Hunt (Lippincott)
Abraham Lincoln, Friend of the People. Clara Ingram Judson (Follett)
The Story of Appleby Capple. Anne Parrish (Harper)

1952 *Ginger Pye.* Eleanor Estes (Harcourt)

Honors

Americans before Columbus. Elizabeth Baity (Viking)
The Apple and the Arrow. Mary and Conrad Buff (Houghton)
Minn of the Mississippi. Holling C. Holling (Houghton)
The Defender. Nicholas Kalashnikoff (Scribner)
The Light at Tern Rocks. Julie Sauer (Viking)

1953 *Secret of the Andes.* Ann Nolan Clark (Viking)

Honors

The Bears on Hemlock Mountain. Alice Dalgliesh (Scribner)
Birthdays of Freedom, Vol. I. Genevieve Foster (Scribner)
Moccasin Trail. Eloise Jarvis Mcgraw (Coward)
Red Sails to Capri. Ann Weil (Viking)
Charlotte's Web. E.B. White (Harper)

1954 *... And Now Miguel.* Joseph Krumgold (Crowell)

Honors

All Alone. Claire Huchet Bishop (Viking)
Magic Maize. Mary and Conrad Buff (Houghton)
Hurry Home Candy. Meindert Dejong (Harper)
Shadrach. Meindert Dejong (Harper)
Theodore Roosevelt, Fighting Patriot. Clara Ingram Judson (Follett)

1955 *The Wheel on the School.* Meindert Dejong (Harper)

Honors

Courage of Sarah Noble. Alice Dalgliesh (Scribner)
Banner in the Sky. James Ullman (Lippincott)

1956 *Carry On, Mr. Bowditch.* Jean Lee Latham (Houghton)

Honors

The Golden Name Day. Jennie Lindquist (Harper)
The Secret River. Marjorie Kinnan Rawlings (Scribner)
Men, Microscopes, and Living Things. Katherine Shippen (Viking)

1957 *Miracles on Maple Hill.* Virginia Sorensen (Harcourt)

Honors

Black Fox of Lorne. Marguerite De Angeli (Doubleday)
The House of Sixty Fathers. Meindert Dejong (Harper)
Old Yeller. Fred Gipson (Harper)
Mr. Justice Holmes. Clara Ingram Judson (Follett)
The Corn Grows Ripe. Dorothy Rhoads (Viking)

1958 *Rifles for Watie.* Harold Keith (Crowell)

Honors

Gone-Away Lake. Elizabeth Enright (Harcourt)
Tom Paine, Freedom's Apostle. Leo Gurke (Crowell)
The Great Wheel. Robert Lawson (Viking)
The Horse Catcher. Mari Sandoz (Westminster)

1959 *The Witch of Blackbird Pond.* Elizabeth George Speare (Houghton)

Honors

The Family under the Bridge. Natalie S. Carlson (Harper)
Along Came a Dog. Meindert Dejong (Harper)
Chucaro: Wild Pony of the Pampa. Francis Kalnay (Harcourt)
The Perilous Road. William O. Steele (Harcourt)

1960 *Onion John.* Joseph Krumgold (Crowell)

Honors

My Side of the Mountain. Jean Craighead George (Dutton)
America Is Born. Gerald W. Johnson (Morrow)
The Gammage Cup. Carol Kendall (Harcourt)

1961 *Island of the Blue Dolphin.* Scott O'Dell (Houghton)

Honors

America Moves Forward. Gerald W. Johnson (Morrow)
Old Ramon. Jack Schaefer (Houghton)
Cricket in Times Square. George Selden, Pseud. for George Thompson (Farrar, Straus)

1962 *The Bronze Bow.* Elizabeth George Speare (Houghton)

Honors

Frontier Living. Edwin Tunis (World)
The Golden Goblet. Eloise Jarvis Mcgraw (Coward)
Belling the Tiger. Mary Stolz (Harper)

1963 *A Wrinkle in Time.* Madeleine L'Engle (Farrar)

Honors

Thistle and Thyme: Tales and Legends from Scotland.
Sorche Nic Leodhas, Pseud. for Leclaire Alger (Holt)
Men of Athens. Olivia Coolidge (Houghton)

1964 *It's Like This, Cat.* Emily Neville (Harper)

Honors

Rascal. Sterling North (Dutton)
The Loner. Ester Wier (Mckay)

1965 *Shadow of a Bull.* Maia Wojciechowska (Atheneum)

Honors

Across Five Aprils. Irene Hunt (Follett)

1966 *I, Juan de Pareja.* Elizabeth Borton De Trevino (Farrar)

Honors

The Black Cauldron. Lloyd Alexander (Holt)
The Animal Family. Randall Jarrell (Pantheon)
The Noonday Friends. Mary Stolz (Harper)

1967 *Up a Road Slowly.* Irene Hunt (Follett)

Honors

The King's Fifth. Scott O'Dell (Houghton)
Zlateh the Goat and Other Stories. Isaac Bashevis Singer
(Harper)
The Jazz Man. Mary Hays Weik (Atheneum)

1968 *From the Mixed-Up Files of Mrs. Basil E. Frankweiler.*
E.L. Konigsburg (Atheneum)

Honors

Jennifer, Hecate, Macbeth, William Mckinley, and Me,
Elizabeth. E.L. Konigsburg (Atheneum)
The Black Pearl. Scott O'Dell (Houghton)
The Fearsome Inn. Isaac Bashevis Singer (Scribner)
The Egypt Game. Zilpha Keatley Snyder (Atheneum)

1969 *The High King.* Lloyd Alexander (Holt)

Honors

To Be a Slave. Julius Lester (Dial)
When Shlemiel Went to Warsaw and Other Stories.
Isaac Bashevis Singer (Farrar)

1970 *Sounder.* William H. Armstrong (Harper)

Honors

Our Eddie. Sulamith Ish-Kishor (Pantheon)
The Many Ways of Seeing: An Introduction to the
Pleasures of Art. Janet Gaylord Moore (World)
Journey Outside. Mary Q. Steele (Viking)

1971 *Summer of the Swans.* Betsy Byars (Viking)

Honors

Knee Knock Rise. Natalie Babbitt (Farrar)
Enchantress from the Stars. Sylvia Louise Engdahl
(Atheneum)
Sing Down the Moon. Scott O'Dell (Houghton)

1972 *Mrs. Frisby and the Rats of NIMH.* Robert C. O'brien
(Atheneum)

Honors

Incident At Hawk's Hill. Allan W. Eckert (Little, Brown)
The Planet of Junior Brown. Virginia Hamilton (Macmillan)
The Tombs of Atuan. Ursula K. Le Guin (Atheneum)
Annie and the Old One. Miska Miles (Little)
The Headless Cupid. Zilpha Keatley Snyder (Atheneum)

1973 *Julie of the Wolves.* Jean Craighead George (Harper)

Honors

Frog and Toad Together. Arnold Lobel (Harper)
The Upstairs Room. Johanna Reiss (Crowell)
The Witches of Worm. Zilpha Keatley Snyder (Atheneum)

1974 *The Slave Dancer.* Paula Fox (Bradbury)

Honors

The Dark Is Rising. Susan Cooper (Atheneum)

1975 *M. C. Higgins, the Great.* Virginia Hamilton (Macmillan)

Honors

My Brother Sam Is Dead. James Lincoln Collier and
Christopher Collier (Four Winds)
Philip Hall Likes Me, I Reckon Maybe. Bette Greene (Dial)
The Perilous Gard. Elizabeth Marie Pope (Houghton)
Figgs & Phantoms. Ellen Raskin (Dutton)

1976 *The Grey King.* Susan Cooper (Atheneum)

Honors

The Hundred Penny Box. Sharon Bell Mathis (Viking)
Dragonwings. Laurence Yep (Harper)

1977 *Roll of Thunder, Hear My Cry.* Mildred D. Taylor (Dial)

Honors

A String in the Harp. Nancy Bond (Atheneum)
Abel's Island. William Steig (Farrar)

1978 *Bridge to Terabithia.* Katherine Paterson (Crowell)

Honors

Ramona and Her Father. Beverly Cleary (Morrow)
Anpao: An American Indian Odyssey. Jamake Highwater
(Lippincott)

1979 *The Westing Game.* Ellen Raskin (Dutton)

Honor

The Great Gilly Hopkins. Katherine Paterson (Crowell)

1980 *A Gathering of Days.* Joan W. Blos (Scribner)

Honors

The Road from Home: The Story of an Armenian Girl. David Kherdian (Greenwillow)

1981 *Jacob Have I Loved.* Katherine Paterson (Crowell)

Honors

The Fledgling. Jane Langton (Harper)
A Ring of Endless Light. Madeleine L'Engle (Farrar)

1982 *A Visit to William Blake's Inn: Poems for Innocent and Experienced Travelers.* Nancy Willard (Harcourt)

Honors

Ramona Quimby, Age 8. Beverly Cleary (Morrow)
Upon the Head of the Goat: A Childhood in Hungary 1939–1944. Aranka Siegal (Farrar)

1983 *Dicey's Song.* Cynthia Voigt (Atheneum)

Honors

Graven Images. Paul Fleischman (Harper)
Homesick: My Own Story. Jean Fritz (Putnam)
Sweet Whispers, Brother Rush. Virginia Hamilton (Philomel)
The Blue Sword. Robin Mckinley (Greenwillow)
Dr. De Soto. William Steig (Farrar)

1984 *Dear Mr. Henshaw.* Beverly Cleary (Morrow)

Honors

The Wish Giver. Bill Brittain (Harper)
Sugaring Time. Kathryn Lasky. Photographs By Christopher G. Knight (Macmillan)
The Sign of the Beaver. Elizabeth George Speare (Houghton)
A Solitary Blue. Cynthia Voigt (Atheneum)

1985 *The Hero and the Crown.* Robin Mckinley (Greenwillow)

Honors

The Moves Make the Man. Bruce Brooks (Harper)
One-Eyed Cat. Paula Fox (Bradbury)
Like Jake and Me. Mavis Jukes (Knopf)

1986 *Sarah, Plain and Tall.* Patricia Maclachlan (Harper/Charlotte Zolotow)

Honors

Commodore Perry in the Land of the Shogun. Rhoda Blumberg (Lothrop)
Dogsong. Gary Paulsen (Bradbury)

1987 *The Whipping Boy.* Sid Fleischman (Greenwillow)

Honors

On My Honor. Marion Bauer (Clarion)
Volcano. Patricia Lauber (Bradbury)
A Fine White Dust. Cynthia Rylant (Bradbury)

1988 *Lincoln: A Photobiography.* Russell Freedman (Clarion)

Honors

After the Rain. Norma Fox Mazer (William Morrow)
Hatchet. Gary Paulsen (Bradbury)

1989 *Joyful Noise: Poems for Two Voices.* Paul Fleischman (Harper/Charlotte Zolotow)

Honors

In the Beginning: Creation Stories from around the World. Virginia Hamilton (Harcourt)
Scorpions. Walter Dean Myers (Harper)

1990 *Number the Stars.* Lois Lowry (Houghton Mifflin)

Honors

Afternoon of the Elves. Janet Lisle (Orchard)
The Winter Room. Gary Paulsen (Orchard)
Shabanu, Daughter of the Wind. Suzanne Fisher Staples (Random House)

1991 *Maniac Magee.* Jerry Spinelli (Little, Brown)

Honor

True Confessions of Charlotte Doyle. Avi (Orchard)

1992 *Shiloh.* Phyllis Reynolds Naylor (Atheneum)

Honors

Nothing but the Truth: A Documentary Novel. Avi (Orchard)
The Wright Brothers: How They Invented the Airplane. Russell Freedman (Holiday House)

1993 *Missing May.* Cynthia Rylant (Orchard)

Honors

What Hearts. Bruce Brooks (HarperCollins)
The Dark-Thirty: Southern Tales of the Supernatural. Patricia McKissack (Knopf)
Somewhere in the Darkness. Walter Dean Myers (Scholastic)

1994 *The Giver.* Lois Lowry (Houghton)

Honors

Crazy Lady! Jane Leslie Conly (HarperCollins)
Dragon's Gate. Laurence Yep (HarperCollins)
Eleanor Roosevelt: A Life of Discovery. Russell Freedman (Clarion)

1995 *Walk Two Moons.* Sharon Creech (HarperCollins)

Honors

Catherine, Called Birdy. Karen Cushman (Clarion)
The Ear, the Eye and the Arm. Nancy Farmer (Orchard)

1996 *The Midwife's Apprentice.* Karen Cushman (Clarion)

Honors

What Jamie Saw. Carolyn Coman (Front Street)
The Watsons Go to Birmingham – 1963. Christopher Paul Curtis (Delacorte)
Yolanda's Genius. Carol Fenner (Margaret K. McElderry)
The Great Fire. Jim Murphy (Scholastic)

1997 *The View from Saturday.* E.L. Konigsburg (Atheneum)

Honors

A Girl Named Disaster. Nancy Farmer (Orchard)
The Moorchild. Eloise McGraw (Margaret K. McElderry)

The Thief. Megan Whalen Turner (Greenwillow)
Belle Prater's Boy. Ruth White (Farrar)

1998 *Out of the Dust.* Karen Hesse (Scholastic)

Honors
Lily's Crossing. Patricia Reilly Giff (Delacorte)
Ella Enchanted. Gail Carson Levine (HarperCollins)
Wringer. Jerry Spinelli (HarperCollins)

1999 *Holes.* Louis Sachar (Farrar)

Honor
A Long Way from Chicago. Robert Peck (Dial)

2000 *Bud, Not Buddy.* Christopher Paul Curtis (Delacorte)

Honors
Getting Near Baby. Audrey Couloumbis (Putnam)
Our Only May Amelia. Jennifer L. Holm (HarperCollins)
26 Fairmont Avenue. Tomie dePaola (Putnam)

Author/Title Index

Subject/Genre Index

Subjects: Subject headings identify major and supporting themes for the Newbery winners.
Curriculum Connections: Curriculum headings identify projects and activities by broad subject areas, i.e., history or science. The themes addressed in each are given in the project heading.
Genres: Genre headings are included for each Newbery title.

A

abandonment 58
acceptance 45, 50
accidents 55, 58, 89
acronyms 79
adjustment 83
adoption 37, 55
adventure 25, 63, 81, 85
aeronautics 34
Africa 81
African Americans 42, 71, 74
African culture 63
airplanes 34
alcoholism 50
anger 40, 69
animal conservation 79
animal cruelty 28
Appalachia 87
Appalachian life 28
apprentices 85
apprenticeships 66
architecture 77
arranged marriages 60, 81
art 15, 25, 37, 42, 58, 79, 89, 94
arts and crafts 17
aunts 74
avalanches 55
aviation history 34

B

baboons 81
bagpipes 83
banishment 83
baseball 22, 40
belonging 66, 83, 96
betrayal 25
bicycles 34
biography 34, 52
birds 60
birth and birthing 19, 66
bombings 71
bragging 85
brothers 16, 34

brothers and sisters 71, 74, 100
bullies 71, 96, 98
buried treasure 98

C

camels 19
camp 98
careers 67, 86
change 52
changelings 83
character 98
charity 100
Chicago fire (1871) 77
child abuse 69
child prodigy 74
Chinese laborers 55
choices 25, 47, 69
cholera 81
Cinderella 94
civil rights 42, 52, 71
civility 79
cleverness 60
codes 58
comics 40
coming-of-age 19, 96
communication 31
community 50, 89
compassion 14, 40, 50, 89
conformity 47
contemporary issues 17
contemporary realistic fiction 14, 19, 22, 28, 31, 37, 40, 45, 50, 58, 69, 74, 79, 81, 96, 98
contests 79, 100
cooking 100
cooperation 55, 85
coping 87
country life 37
county fairs 100
courage 11, 25, 28, 47, 55, 77, 94, 96
cousins 87
creative dramatics 26
crime 45
criminals 63

cruelty 50
Crusades 60
curiosity 14, 83
current events 20, 48, 64, 78, 82
current issues 69
curses 98
customs 81

D

danger 25
Danish Resistance Movement 11
daydreams 45
death 11, 16, 19, 37, 45, 50, 55, 58, 87, 89, 94
debate 47
deception 45
Denmark 11
depression 37, 40
desert life 19
deserts 98
detectives 63
determination 28, 60
diaries 31, 60
disappearances 87
disasters 77
diversity 81
divorce 40, 79
dogs 28, 79
domestic violence 69
dowries 19
dreams 81
drought 89
drugs 74
Dust Bowl 89
duty 19
dystopian society 47

E

ecology 89
economics 87, 90
education 52
elves 14
England 60, 66

environment 79
ethics 28, 29, 31, 47
euthanasia 47
evil 25
exploitation 55
eyes 87

F

fairies 83
families 16, 19, 22, 40, 45, 47, 87, 89, 92
family life 28, 50, 52, 58, 71
family relationships 11
fantasy 69, 83, 85, 94
farm life 16, 89
fate 83, 94, 98
fathers 58, 92
fathers and daughters 60, 89
fathers and sons 45, 96
fear 14, 47, 69, 81, 83, 92
fires 77, 89
flight 34
folk medicine 60, 66
forgiveness 40
free verse 89
freedom 42, 47, 55, 81, 85
freedom of speech 31
friendship 11, 14, 22, 25, 28, 37, 40, 50, 55, 58, 60, 69, 71, 74, 79, 83, 87, 92, 94, 96, 98
fund-raising 50, 96
futuristic world 63

G

gangs 63
gender roles 19, 25, 52, 60, 66
generosity 100
geography 59
German occupation 11
ghost stories 100
ghosts 42
gifted students 79
gifts 94